In 2015, TalenTrust was named to the prestigious Inc. 5000 list, based on 300 percent revenue growth over the past three years. The team at TalenTrust understands the challenges of leading organizations through rapid growth, and is pleased to serve many on the Inc. 5000 list, including these current and former clients:

- DevelopIntelligence

- E2 Optics

- Equian

- Gibson Athletic

- Homewatch Caregivers

- LINX

- National Corporate Housing

- OpenSymmetry

- SAFEbuilt

Inc. 5000 Companies Praise TalenTrust

"We were impressed with the meticulous, methodical process and tools TalenTrust used, and the results they could demonstrate."

— **Mike McCurdie,** CEO,
SAFEbuilt

"The firm's collaborative and agile approach made TalenTrust a key strategic partner, yielding very strong results. Thanks to their efforts, we have hired several key people in sales, management and consulting, which is absolutely critical to obtain our aggressive growth goals."

— **Ray Wolf,** President,
OpenSymmetry

"We tasked TalenTrust with recruiting candidates who have the attitude and aptitude to take on future management roles within our growing organization but who were also willing to start learning our business in entry-level roles to gain the technical skills needed to excel. TalenTrust listened to our needs and helped us hire over thirty excellent full-time employees."

— **Erik Isernhagen,** President,
LINX

Praise for *Solve the People Puzzle*

"An exemplary business book. It's packed with personal examples, research, and practical advice on one of the toughest challenge organizations face: finding, growing, and keeping excellent people."

– Kim Jordan, Co-Founder,
New Belgium Brewing Company

"Every company wants to attract and keep the people it needs to be successful, but many don't know how. This is a big problem for entrepreneurial companies in rapid growth. One or two bad hires can derail a company and be very costly in terms of lost time, momentum, and money. This book tackles all aspects of the recruitment process and has become required reading for all the CEOs I work with."

– Dr. Jana Matthews, Founding Team Member,
Center for Entrepreneurial Leadership at the Kauffman Foundation,
Director of the Centre for Business Growth
at the *University of South Australia*

"Great Work. I applaud the pragmatic straight talk! If you want to be a senior executive, or if you are a senior executive and want to be successful, read this book and put its principles to work. The content is critical to the future of your people and your organization."

– Major General Joseph August "Bud" Ahearn,
U.S. Air Force Retired

"If you want to grow your business, you need this book. It's great perspective for any business leader who strives to stay ahead of the curve."

– Joe Assell, President and CEO,
GolfTEC

"A timely look at proven ways to recruit, engage, and retain top talent. A critical perspective for decision-makers in high-growth companies and those impacted by their decisions."

– David Mead, President,
The Mead Consulting Group

"I admire the way Kathleen Quinn Votaw emphasizes hiring for attitude first and skill second. If retaining top talent is part of your growth strategy—and it should be—then read this book."

–Tim Wolters, Founder and CEO,
RoundPegg

"This book provides a comprehensive assessment of proven leadership lessons. Various examples help illustrate how to continuously improve as a person, a leader, and an organization."

– Ralph W. Christie, Jr., Chairman of the Board,
Merrick & Company

SOLVE
— THE —
PEOPLE
PUZZLE

SOLVE
— THE —
PEOPLE
PUZZLE

How High-Growth Companies
Attract & Retain Top Talent

Kathleen Quinn Votaw

Advantage®

Published by Advantage, Charleston, South Carolina.
Member of Advantage Media Group.

ADVANTAGE is a registered trademark and the Advantage colophon is a trademark of Advantage Media Group, Inc.

Printed in the United States of America.

ISBN: 978-1-59932-629-0
LCCN: 2015955485

10 9 8 7 6 5 4

This publication is designed to provide accurate and authoritative information in regard to the subject matter covered. It is sold with the understanding that the publisher is not engaged in rendering legal, accounting, or other professional services. If legal advice or other expert assistance is required, the services of a competent professional person should be sought.

Advantage Media Group is proud to be a part of the Tree Neutral® program. Tree Neutral offsets the number of trees consumed in the production and printing of this book by taking proactive steps such as planting trees in direct proportion to the number of trees used to print books. To learn more about Tree Neutral, please visit **www.treeneutral.com**. To learn more about Advantage's commitment to being a responsible steward of the environment, please visit **www.advantagefamily.com/green**

Advantage Media Group is a publisher of business, self-improvement, and professional development books and online learning. We help entrepreneurs, business leaders, and professionals share their Stories, Passion, and Knowledge to help others Learn & Grow. Do you have a manuscript or book idea that you would like us to consider for publishing? Please visit **advantagefamily.com** or call **1.866.775.1696**.

For me, it is all about family.
You are my life and my compass, and every one
of you has a special place in my heart.

This book is dedicated to you, who have contributed most to
the person I've become. Because you believe in me, I know I
can do anything I set my mind to—even write a book!

With love and appreciation to:

—my husband, Andy, and my son, John
—my parents, John and Kay Quinn
—my brothers and sisters and their spouses: John and
Ellen Quinn, Maureen and Peter Tarca, Eileen and
Joe Brown, and Kevin and Nancy Quinn
—my nieces and nephews: Matthew Quinn, Dan Quinn,
Conor Quinn, Pat Quinn, Meaghan Quinn, Kevin Tarca,
Casey Tarca, Elise Brown, Sean Brown, Brendan Quinn,
Elizabeth Quinn, Kelly Quinn, and Timmy Quinn
—my in-laws: Joye Dickens, Marilyn Votaw, and Laura Platt

Truly, I am blessed.

Foreword

I've been referring companies to Kathleen and TalenTrust for years because her approach is totally different and it works. I'm sure you'll find her book thought provoking and a call to action.

I spend countless hours inspiring audiences to take action in the areas of sales and sales management. Based on thirty-plus years of business experience, including several stints as CEO of high-growth companies, I am passionate about the time, effort, and strategies companies need to invest into attracting and retaining clients.

I am also sold on this key concept which Kathleen employs both in her business and in this book: if you want A-players on your team, your company must spend as much time and effort attracting and retaining talented employees as it does on finding and keeping clients. Both investments lead to increased profit.

Kathleen shares my passion and energy for serving high-growth companies, and her focus is on solving the people puzzle.

Congratulations on opening this book. You understand that in order to succeed in today's hyper-competitive business environment, you need to make people much more than an afterthought. Read on!

Jack Daly – JackDaly.net

Table of Contents

Acknowledgments

As I have been reminded repeatedly while completing this, my first book—no woman is an island. I have had what feels like an entire village supporting and inspiring me through the process. The world, including my village, is about relationships, and it is my relationships with talented and caring mentors, friends, employees, and colleagues that make this book possible. I am filled with gratitude for you all.

First, I want to thank my family, especially my husband, Andy, and my son, John, who were ever patient and encouraging. And thanks to my parents, John and Kay Quinn, who have done so much to help me become the person I am today.

Special thanks to Sherry Law, for her eloquence and organization, and to Heather Hope, whose inspiration and dogged determination ensured that this book was published this year and not several years from now.

I would like to acknowledge and thank so many people who have influenced the book and helped shape it:

- mentors David Mead, Jana Matthews, and Eileen Candles

- TalenTrust team, including my executive leaders Darrick Christopher and Eileen Desch

- countless clients and colleagues through Vistage, ACG-Denver, and Colorado Companies to Watch

Preface

"Great vision without great people is irrelevant. If I were running a company today, I would have one priority above all others: to acquire as many of the best people as I could. The single biggest constraint on the success of organizations is the ability to get and to hang on to enough of the right people."

—Jim Collins, *Good to Great*

I've penned this book—and you've opened it—because there isn't an easy solution to the people puzzle. I also wrote it because I love the excitement of helping companies find and keep the talent they need to grow, and grow, and grow—and after fifteen years I have much to share on the subject. I get great satisfaction from reversing "recruitment fatigue," "Girl Friday" mind-sets, and other limitations that keep companies from meeting their growth potential. This is a very personal book based on my years of experience working with CEOs who understand that traditional staffing methods don't work for today's companies. It's directed to C-level executives of high-growth companies who are continuous learners and want to understand how to attract and retain the talent they need to achieve their wildest dreams.

My firm, TalenTrust, serves companies with revenues of $10–$500 million. We help them to develop and implement a predictable process and system for attracting and retaining employees, much like most companies already have in place for *client* attraction and retention. We find that there is often a big gap between the reality of the recruitment process and the expectations of people who are hiring new employees. Most hiring managers assume recruitment is an easy business practice. In reality, it is not. It is very much like a sales process.

We are a professional services firm focused on attraction, engagement, and retention of a company's most valuable assets—its people. We advise client companies on how to manage high growth from a people perspective. At the same time, we know it from experience, as we are ourselves a high-growth company. Many of those we serve are on the Inc. 5000 for high-growth companies, and we proudly join them on that list, based on our three-year revenue growth of 300 percent.

Finding people who love the rapid growth and chaos inherent in expanding companies is a special service of ours at TalenTrust. We know these companies need people who will look at something that did not exist before and create it. Perhaps they will help create in-demand products or services or they will solidify processes that improve performance. This takes a unique personality. Some people just want a job that is rote, where the same thing has been done year-over-year, month-over-month. That is not the situation in high-growth companies. We understand that these companies are evolving and require inventive and flexible employees.

From Then to Now

My own work ethic and my inspiration to start TalenTrust are defined by my family upbringing. I am the youngest of five children from an Irish Catholic family. My father emigrated from County Mayo, Ireland, arriving in the United States at the age of twenty-four with a sixth-grade education and $20 in his pocket. His first job was with Travelers Insurance Company, starting as a printing apprentice and eventually rising to lead the entire printing department. This rise from virtually nothing is what is so amazing about the man and something I continue to admire.

My father might have been successful in life, but he did not make a lot of money. Like my four siblings, I paid for at least half of my college costs. In 1985, during my sophomore year at Emmanuel College, I walked into the Kelly Services staffing agency office in Hartford, Connecticut, and they hired me on the spot. After graduation, I was moved to their Farmington, Connecticut, office, where I met a mentor, Eileen Candels, a wonderful woman who is still at Kelly Services and remains a friend.

Ever since that initial interview, I have chosen to be in the recruitment industry. In addition to Kelly Services, I have worked for Olsten Corporation and other organizations small and large that have helped me on my way. I have run East and West Coast branches for multi-billion-dollar companies. Through it all, I have absolutely loved helping companies achieve their growth objectives by getting the right people on board.

My father's strength and commitment are traits I've tried to model throughout my personal and professional life. To get very personal, I am a thyroid cancer survivor. When I had my son more than fifteen years ago, I was diagnosed with cancer. This life-changing diagnosis meant that I had to reframe everything, all while bringing a newborn into this world.

From a professional standpoint, I have also had a variety of challenges. I could put a lot of sugarcoating around it, but essentially the company I worked for at the time of my cancer diagnosis fired me.

This tough and unfair experience ensured that I created an entirely different kind of company, and for that I am thankful. Imagine, a new baby, cancer, and the loss of a job—all in one swoop. Yet the experience made me grow in strength and compassion.

I have never been open about my firing, until writing this book. We know how painful it is to admit, but over the course of our careers, many of us have been fired. Like Lee Iacocca, we need to use those experiences to affirm our strength and overcome the shame. You may remember that Iacocca was fired from the Ford Motor Company, only to later rebuild Chrysler when it was losing millions of dollars due to recalls, saving thousands of jobs in the process. Every person and company has challenges of one kind or another. It is important to study those challenges and evaluate how we overcome them.

All of these early experiences led to my founding of TalenTrust in 2003. From its inception, TalenTrust has been intentionally disruptive within the stagnant and outdated recruiting industry. Our goals are to make the industry better for all involved and solve business issues sustainably. As examples, we guarantee our work, and we reward our team on client satisfaction instead of basing commissions on the salary of placements, as is the typical standard within the industry. As a result, we have set ourselves up for a very difficult, two-stage sales process, as have many innovative companies. First, we must educate prospective client companies that there is another way, something different from what they have long been led to believe is available in the recruitment field, something more valuable. Only then can we move to stage two and explain our actual services and processes and begin building a relationship.

Things change rapidly in entrepreneurial, high-growth companies, almost on a ninety-day cycle. We love this environment of chaos and constant challenge, and because we are a high-growth company ourselves, we are usually well aligned with our clients. We practice what we preach.

The year the global economy bottomed out, 2009, was brutal for us. It was a time of panic and workforce reductions. I found strength by relying on my own professional network. I used the time to talk to CEOs about what they wanted to experience when working with a recruitment firm.

Sharing My Perspective

After numerous conversations with CEOs during those difficult years and three decades of experience in the recruiting industry, I feel I've learned more than a few things worth sharing. First, you have to know why you are doing what you do, a question few people ask themselves. Second, leaders must value and trust their employees, which is much easier to do when you hire people whose personal values and goals align with those of your company.

To find out what else I have learned about the people puzzle, I invite you to read the rest of this book. It's an executive's guide to attracting, retaining, and engaging the best. And it is meant for you.

Introduction

What is one of the biggest challenges facing American CEOs? According to the Vistage Small Business CEO survey, the answer is hiring the right people to drive growth. Among surveyed CEOs, more than half reported unfilled positions, 46 percent had trouble finding qualified people, and 24 percent had trouble finding candidates with a good cultural fit for their company. Locating, hiring, training, and retaining staff is an important issue for CEOs, with 35 percent citing this issue as their most important. [1] A tightening labor market and rising wages have amplified the importance of this issue. What's the most critical finding from the survey? CEOs said unfilled positions seriously limited the growth of their business.

What Keeps You Up at Night?

We know from talking with leaders and from research that CEOs are worried about talent, and they should be. What part of talent management is keeping *you* up at night? According to Vistage, 55 percent of CEOs report having unfilled positions, some for as long as two years.[2] Most of them realize that they *need* to be searching for candidates on a constant basis and *should* have a pipeline of potential employees ready to step up or over at any point in time. But most don't.

---

1 Vistage, "Q2 2014 Vistage CEO Confidence Index Results Released Today Despite Optimistic Economic News Reported in Survey, Hiring Is a Top Concern," July 1, 2014, www.vistage.com/press-center/press-release/q2-2014-vistage-ceo-confidence-index-results-released-today/.
2 Vistage, "CEO Concerned by Slowdown in Economic Growth, According to Q2 2015 Vistage CEO Confidence Index," July 9, 2015, www.vistage.com/press-center/press-release/ceos-concerned-by-slowdown-in-economic-growth-according-to-q2-2015-vistage-ceo-confidence-index/.

If this describes you, how much is this costing your company in revenue, in customer retention, in lost functionality, and in happy and engaged employees? If your company has unfilled positions, chances are you are producing less revenue than projected. Chances are you have fewer customers too.

I can almost guarantee that if you have unfilled positions, you are going to lose happy and engaged employees because you are stressing them out. There is just too much work for them to do. It's a chronic issue. If companies are not focusing on building a pipeline around candidates and we continue to have 55 percent of CEOs worrying about unfilled positions, then we are in an upside-down business position.

You must make finding and keeping great people one of your top priorities.

In discussions with CEOs of middle-market companies (those with revenues between $10 and $500 million), I heard the same fatigue of the recruiting industry, which many consider a necessary evil. Their needs were not being met; they wanted long-term solutions for attracting and retaining the best and brightest talent, not the transaction-based hiring typical of the $122 billion recruitment industry.

These conversations opened up opportunity for TalenTrust and led me to refocus and create our unique business model. Our model involves a highly predictable process that results in finding, engaging, and retaining the right people to drive growth. Our client relationships typically last two to three years; once processes are in place, we step back, providing advice and support as needed.

Creating Camelot

Hiring the right person can change that person's life as well as your company. People change jobs comparatively often these days but do not necessarily find their career or calling. When this does happen, you have created Camelot. You have people who are fully engaged in the mission of the company, and those people will grow exponentially because they are personally invested in your company's welfare.

It is no longer a job for these people. It becomes a conviction. It becomes a goal. It becomes a mission, with everyone moving in the same direction toward the same objectives. High-growth companies need people whose passion matches that of the company. It is not likely that everyone in the company will be a perfect match, but if your core team is not a match, you will never succeed.

An experience I will never forget is our work with a Boulder company in the process of being sold. We brought in sales and engineering people to get the company in shape before the major transformation. Until we brought him in, one gentleman had believed he could never get another job. He asked me point blank, "Do you think they'll hire me? I'm fifty-five years old." My response? "Well, you've got the credentials. Why wouldn't they hire you?"

Candidates burden themselves with so many filters! (And, by the way, so do companies.) This job, working for this company, absolutely changed this man's life. He continues to travel to China and many other locations, using the credentials that some companies would have overlooked, to expand the company into new markets. His wife travels with him (another no-no for some companies), so they can enjoy this new chapter of their life together. Most importantly, the company is growing exponentially. The original owners of the company could not have achieved the sale without this talented and passionate man.

… and this is just one small example of what the right hire can do.

What's Wrong with the Old Ways of Hiring?

The old ways of hiring do not incorporate reliable methods that ensure the right people are hired for the right positions.

Entrepreneurial and high-growth companies are constantly evolving, not realizing how badly they need the processes and systems that will allow them to focus on their core competency. The lack of processes and systems around people is one reason that many of them are in pain as they try to grow.

Many managers begin the hiring process by tapping friends and family. It looks something like this: Manager Joe picks up the phone, calls his friend Bob, and asks for a recommendation to fill an open position. Bob may be a nice guy but probably doesn't have the knowledge to recommend the right person for the job. Nevertheless, Joe hires Bob's contact because he needs someone right now. Most entrepreneurs and small business owners quickly realize they cannot continue hiring this way. They need the *right* people for the *right* roles as the company goes into rapid-growth mode.

That means *never* hiring a candidate in isolation and *always* having multiple candidates, so you have a basis of comparison that allows you to make the best choice for your company. It requires a well-thought-out process to get to the best choice. The sooner companies get to that realization, the less pain they will experience.

Candidates Are in Control

Companies are no longer in the driver's seat. Millennials, in particular, want to "feel" what your company is like before they will even consider an interview. People have choices. Gone are the days when jobs were hard to find. That was in 2008, 2009, and 2010. Now jobs are plentiful, and people are marketable—and they should be well into the future. Candidates have more control, and companies need to court them differently.

Let me give you an example. I recently spoke with a representative at a payments company that is having a tough time attracting the right people and is fearful of disappointing its customers as a result. I was introduced to the senior director of human resources. Given her title, it would be natural to assume that she is a senior person in the company. Yet she began our conversation by saying, "I can't wait. I'm getting yelled at by the chief sales officer who thinks I should have these jobs filled now." Just by hearing this, I knew that at least one of the company's problems was that the people who were driving recruitment efforts did not understand effective recruitment strategies. Imagine, the senior director of HR was recruiting the company's most valuable assets while under pressure and without an effective process or strategy.

I wish I could say this was the first time I had come across this situation. This is not the way to run a company, especially as it grows and needs talent to keep the expansion on track.

Key Takeaways

As you read through this book, my hope is that you'll take away new perspectives on:

- keeping your employees engaged so they don't leave

- cultivating new hires—Always Be Cultivating (ABC) by thinking of recruitment as a sales process

- attracting people who will thrive in your demanding, uncertain, entrepreneurial environment

- hiring for attitude and cultural fit first, and parting ways quickly if the fit isn't right

Stop pretending it is easy. Start being strategic. Give recruitment and retention just as much focus as your customer attraction strategy. Until you do, you will be behind the curve, and that is no good for your company, your current employees, or especially, your bottom line.

My goal in writing this book is to help you to attract and retain your most valuable assets so they can help you succeed.

CHAPTER 1

Let Go of Your Ego

I've got news for you! Unless you are a highly regarded company *with a unique culture, like Google, Zappos, GE, or Marriott, most people are not dying to work for you. In fact, they might not even know you exist, even though your company may be the center of your world.*

I expect company leaders to be proud, however, they must ask themselves the same questions outsiders are thinking, such as: "What makes your company so great? Why would people want to come to work for you? What's your story?"

Hiring is no longer a one-way street as it was in the past. In fact, you may need to take a back seat to the A-players—the employees you want most who are usually in the driver's seat. Gone are the days when employees were grateful to have a job. It is now a mutually beneficial relationship. More than ever, today's employees have a choice.

We experienced that choice ourselves recently as TalenTrust interviewed for someone in business development. Each of our candidates was also interviewing with two other companies. As much as I wanted them to choose us, I knew how arrogant it was for me to think that they would just choose TalenTrust without good reason.

At the same time we were doing our own search, we were helping a consulting firm in Austin that extended three offers to candidates we presented to them. All three offers were declined. This upset our client, who was looking to take off some personnel pressure by filling those three positions. We had to go back to them and help them understand why these people declined the opportunity. Was it culture, was it management, was it vision, was it compensation, or all of the above? Those questions must be considered if you want to become the top choice for your top candidates.

Attract Candidates as You Would Customers

If you want the A-players, your company must spend as much time and effort on attracting candidates as it does on attracting clients. Both investments lead to increased profit. One of your first tasks should be making sure that your company is visible in the marketplace to prospective employees and customers. In the case of the job marketplace, we are referring to both people looking for jobs and those who are open to other opportunities in spite of being gainfully employed. Some of the best people are already busy, doing great work. They are making money for other companies. How are you going to get their attention? How are you going to get them to notice your small or midsized company when there are so many of them out there?

A case in point is a company in the expense reduction industry with a focus on mobile devices. They decided to bring on four enterprise salespeople. Good salespeople, those who can actually sell, are hard to find, and this company expressed the difficulty they were having when we met with them. The company currently earns somewhere between $10 and $50 million in revenue and is growing rapidly, but no one knows anything about them. They are far from a household name. When people recognize a company's name, that alone is a big advantage when it comes to recruiting, but this company is like most others: an unknown. How are they going to compete for A-players, the people with choice?

They have to start focusing on this mind-set: What is in it for the person I am talking to, the candidate we want to work for us? What kind of meaningful work are we doing that can resonate with the generations that are coming into the workplace?

Gravity Payments, based in Seattle, is an example of a company that succeeded in moving to known from unknown. The CEO, Dan Price, was clearly thinking of both current and future employees when he made an announcement that he would cut his own pay and raise that of all of his workers to at least $70,000. If you watch the business headlines, you have probably heard of Dan Price. But had you ever heard of him before this? Within the first day of this announcement, the company had six hundred applications.

His action may seem a bit extreme, but fundamentally Price was saying to his entire company, "I value you as much as I value me.

You matter as much as I do." That is what people want from their employer. They want to matter. It may sound silly, but just as in a marriage, people want to know they will be a trusted partner and that you are concerned about their well-being.

Bring in New People, New Ideas for Continuous Growth and Innovation

Examples may be the best way to explain how important the right people are to your success.

In Denver, we worked with a manufacturing and distribution company called Mile Hi. The CEO, Kristy Taddonio Mullins, came to us and asked, "How can I find the people who can bring the company forward versus maintaining the status quo?"

With a long history of success, why did she ask us that? It is because high-growth companies hit speed bumps, places where their growth and innovation slow. Key individuals at companies will often make statements such as, "What we did last year is good enough," even when it is clearly not working. They fall into patterns and get stuck in ruts.

When she took over leadership of the company, Kristy refused to accept the status quo. She is an innovator who went out and borrowed the $22 million needed to build a new bakery. She realized that she needed the right people in place to help capture the revenue for that investment and wanted people who could stretch and grow into bigger roles as the company continued to expand. In searching for those A-players, we looked for innovators who were experienced in business and not necessarily from within their industry. This client is successful because she realizes that what is truly important is not doing things the same way you have done them in the past but bringing in people who can see what you have been doing and build upon it.

Another fast-growing Colorado client, Mercury, is a payments processing company founded in 2001. In 2009, Mercury had about two hundred employees and a plan to grow 250 percent over the next three years. CEO Matt Taylor needed to assemble a strategic senior leadership team and add key staff members in order to drive this growth. HR was focused on multiple priorities, stretched to capacity, and dependent on numerous external-staffing vendors for recruiting. This environment could describe many high-growth companies!

With a highly collaborative culture, Mercury looked for a trusted partner to help them build a highly functional team and develop a robust process to manage recruitment internally. After taking time to understand Mercury's business and challenges, TalenTrust helped the company grow by more than four hundred employees over a three-year period based on holistic, scalable, cost-effective solutions. We sought innovative people to propel their growth and also helped Mercury establish a five-person internal recruiting team.

Challenge Your Assumptions and Filters

Like most people, business leaders often make assumptions and use certain filters. It is important to challenge those assumptions on a daily, weekly, monthly, quarterly, or annual basis and remove or adjust those filters. We tend to just accept what is happening in our company as "good," which is the enemy of "great"—as we know from Jim Collins, the author of *Good to Great: Why Some Companies Make the Leap ... and Others Don't.*

Candidates have choices, just as customers have choices. And candidates need to know about who you are as a company and what you are doing to stay relevant. How are you going to attract the best candidates to help grow your company? How are you going to do things differently versus the same way you have always been doing them? How will you know whether you are answering these questions from the perspective of your ego or from your company's reality?

CHAPTER 2

Admit That Your Employees Are Looking

T hree out of four full-time employed workers are open to or actively looking for new job opportunities.[3] While some are active and others are passive, recruiters can now easily find them and attempt to lure them away. What does that mean for you and your company?

Three out of four! Shocking, isn't it?

Even if you are skeptical of statistics and want to believe that your company is different, that it has a positive culture and thoroughly engaged workforce, you must realize that some of your people are unhappy but won't tell you. While you are recruiting for

3 CareerBuilder, "2015 Candidate Behavior Study," Accessed on September 23, 2015, http://careerbuildercommuni-cations.com/candidatebehavior/.

open and hard-to-fill positions, you risk losing a significant portion of your *current* workforce. It is highly likely that a recruiter or head-hunter has called almost all of your people at some point, attempting to lure them away from you and into the ranks of another company.

Let's say a company is looking for four enterprise salespeople across the country. They can go into LinkedIn to do a keyword search and learn everything they need to know about experienced salespeople in any market. Their resumes are posted on LinkedIn, and for the first time ever, that's okay. If you remember the early days of the Internet, if your employer found your resume on Monster.com, they would print it, walk over to you, and say, "I found this on Monster. Are you looking for another job?"

Today's technology allows you to easily browse resumes from a broad swath of potential candidates, but are they the right people to grow your company? You can get resumes all day long, but that does not mean you will get the right person. Doing so takes more analysis and strategic effort—but that discussion is for another chapter.

LinkedIn is the most recognized among many tools for people to list their credentials. Members list their accomplishments, statistics, and all of their contact information for people to see. It is there to say, "I invite you to call me." At any time, internal corporate recruiters and external recruiters have access to virtually everyone with a certain skillset.

With this in mind, you need to constantly be thinking, "How am I treating my people, and what can I do to keep them happy?" Have this conversation now. Do not sit in a conference room with other executives and decide what is best for your employees. Get out of your office and talk to your people about what you can do to retain them.

Communicate with All Employees—Engaged or Not

The employer/employee relationship must evolve into one of solid trust. Right now, people are out there thinking of leaving their company but would never, ever think of telling the employer by saying, "You know this isn't quite working for me," until they have a new job and give two-week notice. Trust can eliminate this conundrum.

Wouldn't it be fantastic if we had corporate cultures that encouraged people to sit down with a manager and honestly say, "I'm not feeling challenged. I'm not feeling valued. I'm not feeling like my skills are being used in the best way," without fear of retribution or termination? How different workplaces would be if people could have those kinds of open discussions!

Employers must be courageous, look at themselves, and create environments that support these conversations. Sometimes, people are in the wrong jobs. If Sally works in sales and she is not producing, perhaps she would thrive as account manager. Sometimes you don't have those roles, and if you don't, then you give your people room to go look for other jobs. When you plan for such critical openings by having these discussions, then you are no longer reacting to a catastrophic situation. You are giving yourself room to be strategic—and giving employees cause to think positively about your company, even though they might leave.

Being strategic allows you to plan. I had an employee early in my career who was visibly unhappy. We were a small office of five people, and it was easy to see the strains by watching her nonverbal communication. I sat her down and asked, "What's wrong?" She told me, "I'm just not happy anymore with the work I'm doing." When I responded with, "Okay, are you going to look for another job?" she was shocked by my directness. "I kind of am," she said. My answer to her was that it was fine, and I suggested, "Why don't we make a deal. You give me two months, and I'll give you two months. You look for a job, and I'll look for your replacement."

It was the most perfect parting because it allowed us to have an important dialogue and take time to plan. Now, is everybody made that way? No, but I have to believe optimistically that more people are wired that way than not. There will always be a few people who are what I call "terrorists" in an organization, people who sabotage and destroy the culture and with whom you cannot have these honest conversations. Yet, from my experience, I believe that at least 80 percent of the workforce would love to be able to be that transparent with their employers.

Can that sort of open conversation stop attrition? Perhaps in a few cases, but I believe that when somebody reaches the point where he or she decides to move on, that person should leave. Counter offers simply do not work. The statistics show that most people who receive a counter offer and decide to stay will still end up leaving anyway within a year. Counter offers are usually a desperation plea on the employer's side. Often when someone says, "Boss, I've got another job. I accepted another offer. It's been great working here. I'm giving you my two weeks," the management team scrambles and says, "Holy crap. I can't lose this person. I'm going to have to do all the work and we don't have anyone to replace him. No one is cross-trained … we're going to lose clients …" It's a fire drill. Then management goes back to the employee who resigned and says, "Hey, we really value you, and because you're leaving, now we want to give you more money."

This person isn't leaving because of money! Survey after survey shows that money is not the number-one reason that people leave. Instead, they leave because they're quitting bad cultures, bad managers, and toxic environments. They quit companies that want to do it the way they have always done it, that don't listen to their ideas. Those are the top reasons people leave. They quit because they are not inspired or aren't able to use their creativity.

If people are leaving, find out why. Ask questions and use this valuable insight to address the issue.

Why Do People Quit?

A report from Grow America compiled research from several sources. The truth is, the majority of people, quitting or not, are currently unhappy in their corporate jobs. A study by Harris Interactive indicates a full 74 percent of people would today consider finding a new job. The most recent Mercer's What's Working study says 32 percent are actively looking.

The reasons for their unhappiness, a recent study by Accenture reports:

1. An unlikeable boss (31 percent)

2. A lack of empowerment (31 percent)

3. Internal politics (35 percent)

4. A lack of recognition (43 percent)[4]

---

4 Hall, Alan, "'I'm Outta Here!' Why 2 Million Americans Quit Every Month (And 5 Steps to Turn the Epidemic Around)," Forbes, March 11, 2013, www.forbes.com/sites/alanhall/2013/03/11/ im-outta-here-why-2-million-americans-quit-every-month-and-5-steps-to-turn-the-epidemic-around/.

Treat Recruitment as a Sales Process

Most companies consistently state that their people are their most valuable assets, but often they don't spend the time, effort, or money needed to find and keep great people—and certainly not the resources they spend acquiring customers. What we find is that companies know what they need to do, but many do not do it.

Sales Pipeline Example

Suspects

Leads

Qualified Prospects

Customers

Candidate Pipeline Example

Current Supply & Demand

Those That Fit Your Culture

Best Few

Offers

Employees

What we find is that many of these companies have a low recognition among candidates. Most CEOs sitting in an office where their company is their kingdom find it surprising that quite often nobody has a clue who they or their companies are.

As Simon Sinek espouses, people don't buy what you do, they buy why you do it. They are interested in what your purpose, cause, or belief is—why your company exists and why anyone should care. This philosophy applies equally to attracting employees and selling products, and it has always guided my work. Companies must be eager to understand what motivates their people as well as their customers in order to understand what questions they need to ask. They must then align those questions with the candidates they are trying to bring into their company.

Therein lies one of the conundrums of industry. Entrepreneurs are busy with the idea of what they are going to do and deliver to their clients. However, they need to also spend time on the experience they deliver to the people who help them serve clients.

The typical company makes client attraction a priority, and they track customer acquisition efforts and costs. For example, they track the number of contacts it takes to get a customer or the number of messages prospects received before recognizing the company's name. They might also track what types of messages work better than others and look at advertising and sponsorship dollars or what the best time is to close a deal.

Your marketing and sales teams may do all of this, but do you know these statistics on the candidate side of your business? Companies must be as cognizant of tracking recruitment statistics because happy candidates lead to happy customers.

You first start by understanding the supply and demand for each open position. Is there a shortage? Are these people working for a few key companies or in certain geographic locations? Then, you determine what messages resonate with these individuals. What will entice them to consider new opportunities? Using this info, you launch a campaign to initially attract their attention and then continue to build and nurture a relationship with them through ongoing touchpoints. And you track your candidate pipeline, including conversion rates/times with candidates, much in the same way you track this information for your client pipeline.

Here is a recent example of what *not* to do: A board member of a multi-billion-dollar company was focusing his conversation with us solely around what in the recruitment field is called *time-to-fill*, the length of time between when a position opens and when a candidate is hired. It is the only thing this company measures when dealing with employment issues. Only by measuring this number does the board think it will fix recruitment. Like so many other leaders, this board member was tied to the past and ignorant of the myriad trends and innovations impacting recruitment right now.

We have another term in the recruitment field, called a *butts-in-seats* mentality, which is related to this time-to-fill factor. There is a perception from senior executives and hiring managers that recruitment should be easy. This thinking is a trap that some managers are falling into: "How could this be hard? There are so many people out of work, aren't there? Of course people are going to work for us."

Let me offer the example of a Minnesota manufacturing company that had an aftermarket sales position open for two years. This position involved capturing additional revenue after the product was installed. The employee's role would be going out and making sure that the customer was happy. This was key to customer retention for this company's products.

This position was tied to additional revenue dollars from customers and ongoing business relationships. These were also expensive, long-term purchases, as the company sold energy turbines and other components. By leaving that position open for two years, this company left revenue on the table. Companies need to fill positions on a consistent basis, pipelining candidates in the way they do when acquiring customers.

New employees are simply not going to be instantly available when you have a crisis. That is not the way it works. You must have a continuous methodology toward recruitment, so new candidates are available when you need them, versus when you are in a crisis.

That crisis might be sooner than you think. Don't forget that your people are engaged in other discussions. Your employees could walk out the door at any time, and I have seen this happen en masse with small companies, which can be devastating.

As a company leader, you must have a plan in place to attract the right people. Then you must focus on making sure that you engage them so your company can continue the growth that you expect.

Advice from Jack Daly for My Company and Yours

About 30 percent of our work at TalenTrust is with the sales and marketing function. This makes sense, since we serve high-growth companies; they want to drive revenue performance, and a good place to start is the sales team.

When hiring salespeople, you have to go deep. Jack Daly, my good friend and sales speaker extraordinaire, says in his book *Hyper Sales Growth*, "My guidance to people in the sales manager's spot is to go deep. Find the inner person. Discover things that you would never learn from the resume. *You can recruit for skills, but you need to hire for attitude.*"

Salespeople are naturally charming—they typically smell good, look good, sound good, and dress well. They are likable people. But do they have the stamina to go the distance and grow your revenue?

Early on with TalenTrust, we brought on a sales leader for a small credit reporting company. His background was not in the industry, but his character, drive, passion, and attitude were so aligned that it worked, and it worked for more than ten years! As a result, the company has more than doubled its revenues and diversified its product offerings.

Too many companies want the *perfect* fit. I have to say, sorry, but there is *no* perfect fit. You have to focus first on attitude and develop your people into great leaders and brand stewards.

CHAPTER 3

Overcome Low Engagement

"Employee turnover rates continue to swell upward. They went up 44 percent in 2014."

—John Sullivan, from ERE.net.[5]

Engagement is an interesting concept. Lots of business owners and those in the C-suite dismiss it as a trendy buzzword. When you understand what it really means, you see that it is where the rubber meets the road; it is where employees begin to adopt an ownership mentality.

Engaged employees look out for one another and for your customers. They make fewer mistakes, and they own their work

5 Sullivan, John, "The Top 10 'Bleeding Edge' Recruiting Trends to Watch in 2015," ERE Media, January 12, 2015, www.eremedia.com/ere/the-top-10-bleeding-edge-recruiting-trends-to-watch-in-2015/.

results. They want to work at your company, and they are more productive. They know what to do, and they understand how they fit into your overall purpose and mission. Engaged employees don't leave, saving you the enormous cost of replacing them.

Unengaged employees, on the other hand, tend to be unhappy or bored at work and are sometimes hostile. They can cost you customers, who are much cheaper to retain than replace, and they undermine your success in a variety of other ways. Far from just a buzzword, engagement is one of the key factors that determine whether you are a good company or a great company.

By increasing engagement, your people are happier, and they stay with you longer. The most common estimate is that it costs on average 150 percent of the salary you pay a person to replace him or her. That is the cost of turnover, which directly impacts your profitability. When you engage your employees, you will save those turnover costs. Engaging employees isn't just a nice thing to do. It makes business sense.

There are tools out there to assess employee engagement, and we'll discuss some in this chapter. But keep in mind that nothing replaces you, the owner or CEO, being in the trenches with your people. Your company will never be too big for you to engage regularly on the front lines. You must take the pulse of what's happening. Engaged employees' willingness to give it their all unlocks your greatest potential for competitive advantage. You cannot afford to remain a spectator.

Gallup Links Engagement to Crucial Business Outcomes[6]

A staggering 87 percent of employees worldwide are not engaged at work. The world has a crisis of engagement—one with serious and potentially long-lasting repercussions for the global economy.

But it doesn't have to be this way. In the 1990s, Gallup's groundbreaking research identified the most important factor in helping companies grow—employee engagement—and developed its influential Q12 survey that included twelve actionable workplace elements that link to revenue growth.

As the pioneer in the employee engagement movement, Gallup has consistently found powerful links between employees who are engaged in their jobs and the achievement of crucial business outcomes. Companies with highly engaged workforces outperform their peers by 147 percent in earnings per share and realize:

- 41 percent fewer quality defects

- 48 percent fewer safety incidents

- 65 percent less turnover (low-turnover organizations)

- 25 percent less turnover (high-turnover organizations)

- 37 percent less absenteeism[7]

6 Gallup, "The Culture of an Engaged Workplace: Q12 Employee Engagement," Accessed on September 22, 2015, www.gallup.com/services/169328/q12-employee-engagement.aspx.
7Gallup, "The Culture of an Engaged Workplace: Q12 Employee Engagement," Accessed on September 22, 2015, www.gallup.com/services/169328/q12-employee-engagement.aspx.

A highly engaged workforce means the difference between a company that thrives and one that struggles. When employees are engaged, they are passionate, creative, and entrepreneurial, and their enthusiasm fuels growth. These employees are emotionally connected to the mission and purpose of their work. When employees are not engaged, they are indifferent toward their jobs—or worse, outright hate their work, supervisor, and organization—and they will destroy a work unit and a business.

Take the Pulse of Employee Engagement

There are many questions you should ask your employees to assess their engagement. It takes courage to ask the questions because you will have to deal with the answers, and it takes a strong commitment to check in frequently. When you ask, you must take action to address any concerns employees raise, even if it means explaining why you cannot do something. Communicate about whatever comes up. Employees will only share their perspective if they trust that you are listening and working to improve their situation.

Survey Your Employees

A variety of surveys can assess engagement, including The Gallup Q12 and Top Places to Work surveys. Another option is RoundPegg, which quantifies people's values and helps companies to guide culture through hiring, development, and engagement. Whatever survey you select, it should be done regularly to account for the peaks and valleys in every employee's lifecycle.

In addition to written surveys, you can conduct regular focus groups on certain engagement topics. There might be a handful of issues you want to know about in your company. Have the courage to ask the questions at every company or every divisional meeting. Hold town hall meetings. What questions do the employees have for the owners of the company? Conduct "pulse surveys" to gain deeper understanding in real time, and try to understand opinions on immediate or critical issues. A great tool is called TINYpulse, which allows you to use mobile technology to ask a quick question of your employees, such as: "How do you feel about the new dress code? How do you feel about the new benefits? How do you feel about our customer retention initiatives?"

All of these tools can be part of the mix, depending on the size of your company, your culture, and your budget. Whenever possible, use open-ended questions, beginning with how, what, why, who, when, or where. You will get more information that way, and you will get a better sense of the strength of the emotions behind the answers. Open-ended questions are practical when you have a small employee population, when you are meeting in person, or when you have the resources to read through and track responses on what can be lengthy answers.

Most traditional surveys consist mainly of "closed-ended" questions that ask respondents to rate their answers based on a three- or five-point scale from strongly disagree to strongly agree. When you have a large employee population or limited resources, closed-ended questions make sense. They measure trends but not much emotion. Many surveys of this type conclude with one or two open-ended questions. Surveys are more reliable when confidentiality is ensured, so consider using outside or third-party resources.

Some of my favorite engagement questions are:

- What has your manager done recently to inspire you?

- What are the most important resources you have to do your job effectively?

- How does your role contribute to achieving business outcomes?

- What makes you trust the information you receive?

- What makes you feel valued for the work that you do?

And my top ratings-based statements are:

- I have the opportunity to do what I do best every day.

- Someone at work encourages my development.

- My opinions matter.

People need to know they matter. Never be afraid to ask the right questions and then take action where it makes sense, or explain why it doesn't make business sense. Always measure the results of what you do with further surveys, focus groups, or discussions.

Check In with Your Customers

Talking to your customers is another way to determine the engagement levels of your employees. When was the last time you, as a CEO, CFO, or other member of the leadership team outside of sales or marketing, actually picked up the phone and talked to your customers? Ask them what it's like to do business with you. Their answers, and examples, will tell you how engaged your people are and also help you better understand their needs.

By creating a culture that supports the well-being of your employees, you will cause a chain reaction that ends in your sustainable business success. Your employees will provide experiences that customers rave about.

"Clients do not come first. Employees come first. If you take care of your employees, they will take care of the clients."

—Richard Branson

Develop Your Staff

"Anyone who stops learning is old, whether at twenty or eighty. Anyone who keeps learning stays young. The greatest thing in life is to keep your mind young."

—Henry Ford

This book is about the continuous learning we all need to do as leaders. By the same token, we need to continuously encourage our people to learn—and put money behind that learning. Have you thought about your budget for training and development? Often, professional development only becomes part of the plan when we are about ready to let somebody go. It is used as a last-resort proof of concept. What if we started doing it proactively for the purpose of engaging and keeping our people and teaching them things that they want to learn? The *lack* of professional development is one of the primary reasons people choose to leave. The gift of professional development creates a sense of security, well-being, and appreciation for your employees.

Training does not have to be expensive. It can be as simple as a well-defined and executed mentoring program. Even if you don't have mentors within your company, you know people in the business community who can serve as mentors for your people. Be creative, and consider what resources you already have access to but aren't using.

When you have budget constraints, training should be the last thing you cut. Underfunding or reducing your training in either good or bad times can put your business at risk because people will not feel valued. I hear time and again in all kinds of situations that people are a company's most valuable asset. If you believe that is true, invest first in your people so they know you value them. From there, they will take care of you.

In my own company, I have found that putting dollars into professional development has helped create a curious group of people who keep asking questions and innovating. Development has meant outside coaching for some of our highest performers and specific training for more technical people. In either circumstance, they have raised their hand and said, "Hey, I'm interested in this training," and we have found the dollars. It has paid off for them and for TalenTrust every time.

Connect Personal and Professional Growth

Professional growth enables personal growth and vice versa. Both build self-confidence, which helps people to become more adaptable and less risk averse—the kind of people we want in our companies. Everyone has filters. Everyone has attitudes and beliefs that they bring with them into the workplace. If you invest in professional growth and challenge your people's intellects, it makes people more flexible and more curious. When they become more curious, they will also seek better solutions for your customers, and they will ask more questions, versus following the script that they have acquired somewhere along the way.

To personalize development, ask your employees what interests them. What do they want to learn about that is relevant to your company? Training and development should have an alignment with your company, your business, your process, and your products. Make training relevant, personal, and motivating. That way, everyone wins.

Fortune Highlights the Value of Training

Training has been shown to significantly increase profits for companies, according to *Fortune Magazine*, which examined the issue in their 100 Best Companies survey. A 2015 article stated, "First, the best workplaces are getting better. Because Great Places to Work has used the same rigorous methodology to identify the nation's best employers for nearly two decades, we can make comparisons. Take education and development, for example. In 1998 the average amount of training for managers and professionals was 41 hours, while hourly and administrative staffers received 33 hours. This year the numbers were 78 and 94 hours, respectively, which is nearly 80 percent higher."[8]

Focusing on training and development:

- ensures that people can do their jobs effectively

- increases employee motivation

- increases efficiencies in processes and systems

- inspires innovation in strategies and products

- cross-trains between departments and across regions (a safety net when you lose staff)

- lowers risk management (in areas like sexual harassment and diversity)

- increases productivity

- improves customer relationships

- helps to maintain a competitive advantage

Jack Welch, the former CEO of General Electric and business book author, has said, "An organization's ability to learn and translate that money into action rapidly is the ultimate competitive advantage, so what are you doing to help your people learn?"

8 Moskowitz, Milton, and Levering, Robert, "The Best Employers in the U.S. Say Their Greatest Tool is Culture," Fortune, March 5, 2015, http://fortune.com/2015/03/05/best-companies-greatest-tool-is-culture/.

Consider When and How to Train

Training should be ongoing. It begins at the onset of your thirty- to ninety-day onboarding process to ensure employees are well informed, confident, and competent to start their job. It continues so that you develop as many A-players as possible; the ones who never stay with the status quo; the ones who demand the opportunity to learn, grow, and progress; the people you cannot afford to lose.

Training and development are also at the heart of a solid succession plan. Otherwise, when Joe and Anna leave your company, what are you going to do? You risk losing their corporate knowledge and their clients. When you have a training plan—including redundancy in case employees suddenly leave—you have fewer worries. In addition to planning for the unexpected, training and development give you the flexibility to ask Joe and Anna to move on if they are not performing to expectation. This can revolutionize how you run your organization.

Training can take many forms. Not every form is right for every employee. People learn differently. Some people are comfortable sitting through a PowerPoint presentation and clicking at their leisure. Others would hate sitting in a room alone and clicking a button for training. Some people relate to a talking head; some like self-guided online training; some prefer face-to-face. It goes back to knowing the person you are hiring. How does he or she learn best? Ask and you will know. Developing a flexible training and professional development program will help you tailor your approach based on your employees' needs and preferences.

Inspire Loyalty and Retention

The old adage "Leave your personal life at home" is no longer applicable, if it ever was. Work or play, everything is personal. Who doesn't like to be complimented, remembered, and respected at home or at work? If you still have the mind-set, "I don't want to know too much about you; leave your personal life at the door," you should just shut this book and put it down. You are wasting your time. There is nothing in the world like recognition from a boss who notices the milestones and other events in your life.

I am a big proponent of noticing. For example, we recently celebrated the pregnancy of one of our employees from the time we heard until the time she gave birth. When I later saw her at a company function months later and asked, "Hey, how's the baby? How's the move? How's everything going?" I got a lovely note from her afterward saying, "Thank you so much. I can't believe you remembered. I appreciate it very much."

Another time, we flew in an employee who works for us out of Texas for an event. I received a beautiful thank-you note from her saying that she loves working with a company that values its employees and is looking forward to building relationships with everybody on the team. Making sure she was present for the event was a worthwhile investment on our part. Now I know that she is completely engaged in what we are trying to do, even though she works several states away.

Sincere interest and acknowledgment are inspirational for everyone, from the CEO to everyone else in the company and back. Pay attention to what most people would call the small things. They are big.

TalenTrust isn't unique in recognizing these issues. According to Target Training International, 60 percent of customers stop dealing with companies because of an employee's perceived indifference.[9] It is the same with employees and management. According to Bain & Company, a top-management consultant firm, the average company loses 20–50 percent of its employee base each year because of employee indifference.[10] This is a real problem. People want to be inspired and motivated, and great leaders spend a good portion of their time focusing on employee happiness. How about you?

Employees Can't Engage without Trust

If you take care to hire the right people, you can trust that they will do the right thing. Trust is a topic that is top of mind for me after recently speaking with the CFO of a $150-million company with an eighty-person sales force. They were growing rapidly and were set to move to a larger, more expensive location. My suggestion was not to move the entire sales force to the new facility, but instead, let them work virtually. I was shocked by the CFO's response. He said, "No, because I don't trust them."

So if the CFO of the company does not trust his sales force, I am certain that none of those eighty salespeople trust him, either. You need to trust the people you hire to do the job you give them. Give them the career path. Give them the training. Make sure your managers know what to do, and give them the license to create

9 Michael, Nancy. "Customer Loyalty: Elusive, but Critical: To Create a Cadre of Customer Advocates, Focus Your Efforts on 'The Three Rs'," *ABA Banking Journal* 99, no. 2 (February 2007).
10 Matriz CX, "The Top 11 Ways to Increase Your Employee Loyalty," Accessed on September 22, 2015, www.maritzcx.com/wp-content/uploads/2014/11/MCX-11-Ways-Employee-WP.pdf.

"wow" experiences for your customers. It is remarkable to me that this company would rather pay more in rent than toward rewarding the behavior that they want in people. To me, it is downright nuts.

It all goes together. Customer loyalty and employee loyalty are locked in a web of interconnectivity. They are two sides of one coin. If your employees do not think well of you, then they are not going to do a great job, and they are not going to treat your customers with respect. Your customers, in turn, will go elsewhere.

A Word about Hourly Employees

Your hourly employees may matter the most. You might say, "Well who cares? It's an hourly job, easily replaced, a cashier ... a server ... " But they are often closest to your customers.

So why do hourly workers at Nordstrom go out of their way to make sure your experience is exceptional? Engagement—and it does not have to be expensive. Most Nordstrom workers are hourly employees, even if some make commission. However, all of them, from top to bottom and everywhere in between, know that customer interaction is key. Their values are aligned with customer service, as are the company's overall goals. That person completing your purchase of a package of underwear is going to make sure you are really happy with your purchase. He or she might also ask, "Did you think about socks?" They are trained to think one step ahead. Nordstrom puts a lot of money behind training people, so they know what to do next and how to treat customers.

This extra training also results in add-on sales for the company at the register. Once customers are in the store and shopping, the extra money management puts into training means that the company gets more out of those customers because of their well-trained and happy sales-people. How does your customer experience compare? How do you show your hourly employees that they are valued?

CHAPTER 4

Don't Mind the Gap

Those "kids with their phones," as managers often disparagingly refer to millennials, are likely your employees and customers. They are our future and the future of your company. Statistics indicate that 50 percent of the global workforce will be of the millennial generation by 2020.[11]

There is a generation gap in the workforce only in terms of perception. Because people are working longer, out of necessity or choice, there are now four generations working together for the first time in our history. What can we learn from each other? How can we keep from rushing to judge? How do we work together in harmony and avoid conflict?

---

11 PwC, "Millennials at Work: Reshaping the Worplace," 2011, www.pwc.com/m1/en/services/consulting/documents/millennials-at-work.pdf.

It is dangerous to label any group, and I caution people to stop joking about the generations. Everyone brings gifts to the party. Business leaders should be the first to model a focus on the positive attributes that every generation contributes, valuing and embracing everything from the traditional ways of doing things to change and innovation, whenever it fits the specific situation. Evaluate and adapt.

Stop Ignoring Millennials

Like the generations before them, millennials are bright, wonderful people whose qualities can breathe new life into your company—and they are probably more maligned than any previous generation of workers.

Unlike with past generations, too many companies look at millennials as presenting obstacles rather than opportunities. To define them, millennials are roughly those born since 1980, reaching college about the time of the 2000 millennium, with the oldest now reaching their midthirties. By 2020, millennials will represent about 50 percent of the global workforce, the largest segment of workers. They are a source of growth and expansion for your company.

Companies should be developing strategies to attract the bright, eager, intelligent, capable, hardworking millennials who will attract like-minded customers. These people are already working in and leading US companies, with 15 percent of them already in management positions, according to PayScale.com.[12] A 2015 study by Elance-oDesk showed that currently millennials represent 27 percent

---

12 PayScale Human Capital, "Gen Y in the Workplace," Accessed on September 22, 2015, www.payscale.com/gen-y-at-work.

of managers, 5 percent of senior managers, and 2 percent of executives in American companies.[13]

These millennials want to grow with your company. They want to do meaningful work. How are you connecting growth and meaning to the work at your company? What is going to attract millennials to your company, your products, and your services?

Don't Filter Out

People filter out others for the silliest things—forming lasting opinions within the first few seconds of meeting someone. By overcoming your biases, you will open yourself to welcoming in people who could potentially help you grow your business.

The millennial generation, with its commitment to free expression, seems to offer companies numerous reasons to filter them out. Millennials like to express themselves through things like hair color, tattoos, and unique clothing. Most hiring managers approached by a candidate wearing jeans and a flannel shirt and sporting tattoos and orange hair would consider that person a punk—but they would probably be wrong. That "punk" might be the brightest kid on the block and could possibly be a major game changer in your organization. But, instead, he or she may get welcomed in by a competitor and be creating success for them instead of you.

Perhaps one of the best examples of this is "Mohawk Guy," Bobak Ferdowsi, the MIT-educated NASA scientist who became a sort of celebrity during the Curiosity space landing. It is hard to find someone smarter than a real live rocket scientist, and if all NASA

---

13 Elance-oDesk, "The 2015 Millennial Majority Workforce: Study Results," October 2014, http://elance-odesk.com/millennial-majority-workforce.

saw was his hair and filtered him out, NASA would have lost a great employee. We need to embrace people's differences and diversity through engaging with people in all walks of life, including people of different generations.

On the other end, millennials could be judging managers or coworkers as old, fat, white men wearing suits and ties or women in pant suits and shoulder pads as totally dated and uncool. It can go both ways—with neither generation appreciating the intellect and value that the other contributes.

We all have filters, and they can be necessary and useful, but we have to be very careful about how we process people through those filters. It is to a company's advantage to help employees bridge generational perception gaps. As an example, create internship or mentorship programs that can help eliminate filter-out thinking such as, "This person won't fit in my workplace culture, because he/she doesn't look like me." More seasoned workers and millennials could work together in these programs and experience the value of their differences.

The LINX Gold Star Example

One of our customers, LINX, needed a solution around something quite vague. LINX is a technology integrator specializing in the design, installation, and support of network cabling systems, multimedia systems, and security systems, and the CEO believes in growing people from the ground up. He came up through the ranks himself and so did many of his leaders. His question to us was, "Why

aren't more people willing to pay their dues by climbing the ladder, starting at the bottom rung?"

He was experiencing high turnover and needed a plan to attract and engage the right type of person: millennials with some work experience in the trade who want to work with their hands and—most important—are hungry to learn and grow.

We agreed to a ninety-day pilot and got busy designing a solution for attracting these types of people. We began by spending many hours with company leaders to define the ideal candidate, focusing on work-related criteria and perhaps more importantly on attitudes, beliefs, and cultural fit. Values matter greatly to the CEO. We began slowly with only five positions, and I am happy to say that LINX now has more than thirty trainable, grateful, hard-working millennials on its team.

Millennials were the desired solution for this client, and because they are young, it is expected that they will need training. However, no matter what generation your employees are a part of, training should be at the heart of your program because it demonstrates that you are serious about retaining your people. They will know from day one that they are valued.

Millennials Have Global Perspective, Accept Diversity

The millennial generation is probably the most diverse that we have ever had. The millennial generation is engaged with a global world. This is in contrast to the more seasoned generations that have until now focused on the world right around them.

For millennials, it is not unusual to jump online and connect to Africa, India, or anywhere in the world to see what's happening and engage in a variety of ways. Millenials are connected globally through critical topics of hunger, politics, education, and more. The world is coming to them in ways that older generations have never experienced. Young people today create their own realities—and they accept the diversity they experience everywhere in their digital journeys.

Can millennials encourage seasoned colleagues to embrace more diversity in the way we think, walk, talk, and dress and accept differences in our political affiliations, religious beliefs, and sexual orientation? Can seasoned employees help the millennial generation to understand and learn from the past? It is important to understand, with compassion, that we come to the table with different experiences. Through communication, we can bridge those differences if we all come to the table with an open mind.

Business leaders can and should be catalysts in fostering understanding. Companies with business models built to cater only to those now in their forties, fifties, and sixties will not survive. As current customers age out, companies run by the more-seasoned generations need to plan how to serve a greater number of millennials.

Our business models need to shift in order to respond to the needs of these new customers rather than focus on our needs as owners.

Millennials Embrace Technology, Expect Transparency

With their understanding of complex technology, millennials are valuable agents of change and growth. If you empower them to make good choices about technology and social media for your company, you can grow exponentially. Millennials understand and adapt to technology in general, and they are talented communicators on social media. Imagine the positive impact this can have on your company and your profits.

With technology comes greater transparency. While millennials embrace a more transparent world, many in the seasoned generations are scared to death of it. Someone blogging about our internal workings? No way! These days, it is not simply companies evaluating applicants—it is also applicants evaluating prospective employers. Facebook, LinkedIn, Glassdoor, and other social media sites mean that neither side can hide. Connections and opinions are available with a simple click. Millennials want to know everything about a company or industry before they accept a job, and they will work for a company only as long as it is mutually beneficial. For millennials, a job is much more than punching a clock and getting a paycheck.

Being transparent means sharing information—the good, the bad, and the ugly. Encourage it, don't hide from it. This is how everyone in the company can move forward toward solutions. Millennials want to know that they are joining a strong culture with values that align with theirs. This is important to them. While you are checking their references, they are out there checking your reputation. You can see pictures of them. They can see pictures of you. When you walk into a meeting with them, they already know what you look like, long before you have met face-to-face.

To give you an example, Glassdoor has been perceived as a portal for disgruntled employees. To counteract the negative information posted there, brave CEOs who are confident in their cultures could say to employees: "Look, some people who have left the company have posted negative or untrue messages about us on Glassdoor. This is your company! I encourage you to get on Glassdoor or Indeed and talk about your experience here. Tell the truth, no need to lie. We know we aren't perfect, but why don't you share your experience? If the seat next to you is unfilled, it might be because candidates are making their decisions based on false perceptions on social media. Tell the full story. Make sure your voice is heard, too."

TalenTrust is a case in point. We are not exempt from challenges with turnover and getting our cultural hiring right. If you review our Glassdoor ratings, there are negative comments from prior employees. Instead of burying it, we brought the information to our team and asked them to make their voices heard by posting their own reviews. This has made a big difference as we all pulled together to overcome the negative feedback. If you are concerned about what your employees might say about the company, take a close look at your culture.

Remember the Tylenol scare? It was bravery and transparency through that crisis that saved Johnson & Johnson when the company was attacked. The point is that you have more to gain from embracing transparency than being afraid of it.

Technology also helps millennials find companies that meet their high expectations for personal satisfaction and social good, which are different expectations from previous generations. Millennials want jobs that are valuable to their personal growth and that help them foster a meaningful connection to their work. There is a large wave of companies based on social entrepreneurship—the attempt to draw upon business techniques to find solutions to social problems. For example, for every pair of shoes they sell, TOM'S Shoes gives one pair of shoes to a child in need. That is a very simple example from one of the most popular social enterprises.

What is your company doing to help those who are disadvantaged? The millennial generation wants to do meaningful, purposeful work that touches people's lives. How can you offer meaningful work for the millennials—or add a social component to employment, like time off for employees to volunteer? Whatever "good" you do in your products or services or in the community, post it online for millennials to find when they are evaluating your organization.

In the end it is all about all generations working together. Bridge the gaps. That is how you make a great company that will last through many generations.

"There are precious few Einsteins among us. Most brilliance arises from ordinary people working together in extraordinary ways."

—Roger Von Oech

CHAPTER 5

Understand It's *Not* about the Beer

"The secret of my success is that we have gone to exceptional lengths to hire the best people in the world."

—Steve Jobs

They're not here for the beer—and you wouldn't want them if they were. It could be a beer tap. It could be a foosball table. But what your employees are really happy about is the atmosphere, the culture within a company that created that special perk. Walt Disney was right when he said, "You can design and create and build the most wonderful place in the world, but it takes people to make the dream a reality." That's how he created The Happiest Place on Earth. That philosophy can help you build a happy company.

I was at a Vistage meeting presenting trend data on leadership, hiring, and engagement when one of the CEOs asked me, "Do you really think it's about the beer? You know, I've got a beer tap, I've got a foosball table. Is that going to attract people?"

"It's not about the beer," I said. "It's about how you treat people and the experience they have working in your organization. That's what will create a culture that attracts and retains talent." All of those little things are good, but the company culture underneath the beer is paramount. You have to create a culture in which individuals can thrive.

The *Fortune* "100 Best Companies" surveys clearly show that workplace culture can be a competitive advantage for companies. The most recent listing showed that since 1998, the "100 Best Companies have outperformed the S&P 500 index by a ratio of nearly 2 to 1," according to a study by the Russell Investment Group. *Fortune* points to well-known companies like Google, which has been the number-one company in the listing six times in the past eight years. Google's management knows that their corporate culture impacts the bottom line in a positive way, ensuring that they get the best of the A-players out there. *Fortune's* research "puts to rest the old notion that treating employees well might hurt the bottom line."[14]

Special benefits like beer and foosball serve as illustrations of what your culture allows. What people are looking for from their company's culture these days are things such as flexibility, feeling valued, and creatively working with interesting people in a dynamic atmosphere. These are the kinds of things that make employees happy. And who is going to leave a company that makes them happy?

---

14 Moskowitz, Milton, and Levering, Robert, "The Best Employers in the U.S. Say Their Greatest Tool Is Culture," Fortune, March 5, 2015, http://fortune.com/2015/03/05/best-companies-greatest-tool-is-culture/.

Study the Elements of Today's Great Workplace Cultures

You can't cover up an unhappy culture with beer. If your company is still operating with a static culture brought over from the twentieth century, it is time to change. There are several things that every twenty-first-century workplace culture should offer employees, with their own unique spin, of course. Among the most important are fun, flexibility, and crazy-good perks—underpinned by purpose, guidance, and trust.

Fun—It Shouldn't Be an Afterthought

Barbara Brannen, who runs a company called Playmore, is an expert in injecting playfulness and fun into business culture. She believes that by creating an atmosphere where people can laugh together, you can create a place where people want to work—and that attracts the A-players. You won't have to work so hard to get people to apply for your job openings. Fun facilitates communication, which means people get along better, which results in better decisions and more innovation. All of this leads to increased motivation and productivity and less stress. And your customers will ultimately be much better served. Play is not fluff. It flows to your bottom line.

Still, the fun must reflect your organization's values and the assumptions that define behavior in your workplace. You don't want fun to be disruptive or replace productivity. Make fun a company value, and hire people who believe that fun is necessary and positive.

Flexibility—Without It You May Survive, But You Won't Soar

If you want to attract a pipeline of candidates, offer as much flexibility as you possibly can. We see every day that this is critically important to most of today's employees. They are looking for flexibility and a better work-life balance. The best twenty-first-century companies are focusing on the needs of employees. Creative work alternatives translate into big wins for everyone. Engaged employees bring both their heads and hearts to work. Simply put, employees cannot be expected to check their lives at the door anymore, as if they ever could. You hire the whole person. When you hire new employees, you hire their family and community and all that they entail.

A prime example of inflexibility and old-fashioned thinking is the large percentage of employers who don't trust that employees will really work if they are out of sight. This creates a huge and unnecessary issue for candidates. More studies than I can count show that people working from home are more productive, including a nine-month study described in a 2014 *Harvard Business Review* that found that not only did home-based employees make 13.5 percent more calls than those working on site, but companies also saved on average $1,900 on space and furniture per employee during that period.[15]

Working virtually is a huge benefit to many of your employees and can be to your company as well. Among the things you can do to improve your culture and focus on the needs of employees is to embrace the work-from-home concept. Cisco does it, Deloitte does it, and Google does it. In 2015, FlexJobs, which lists companies

15 Bloom, Nicholas, "To Raise Productivity, Let More Employees Work from Home," *The Harvard Business Review* (Jan-Feb 2014), https://hbr.org/2014/01/to-raise-productivity-let-more-employees-work-from-home.

that allow employees to work from home, showed that the top one hundred companies they analyzed had a 26 percent increase in the number of remote jobs posted over the last year.[16] These companies are competing for the same people you are, and they're attracting many higher-quality people because they let them work virtually. If they can do it, except in exceptional circumstances like emergency or retail, *you* can do it on a smaller scale. Allowing employees to work from home or other remote locations can increase productivity and profits. It also greatly enhances trust.

What happens when you have that kind of trust with your employees who work remotely? We have a woman on our team, for example, who has family in New York. She lives in Colorado where TalenTrust is located. Three weeks out of the year, she bundles up her company phone and laptop and heads out to New York to work from there. As long as she gets the work done, why do I care whether she's working from New York or in Colorado? This allows her to go to dinner with her family and to play with her nieces and nephews. All of this creates great loyalty between the company and her, and it provides freedom for her to lead a full life her way. Hire adults and trust them.

I should add that trust is built on setting and managing clear expectations. If, as part of the hiring process, you immediately create a structure that doesn't promote trust, like imposing a "big brother is watching" mentality, you will undoubtedly generate suspicion followed by consequences when expectations are predictably not met.

What if you did it in reverse, instead telling new hires: "I trust you. I believe in you. I hired you for your credentials and my belief that you can lead this operation or function. Here's your job. Go do

---

16 Weller Reynolds, Brie, "100 Top Companies with Remote Jobs in 2015," FlexJobs, January 20, 2015, www.flexjobs.com/blog/post/100-top-companies-with-remote-jobs-in-2015/.

it. Let's check in once a week. I can help you navigate, serving as your mentor or coach." This method is much more successful at building trust than is the more common approach of: "This is the way you're going to do it. This is the way we do things, here. This is a checklist." Think of all the creativity that is destroyed by such an attitude.

There are other less-common strategies to create flexibility, for example:

- You could permit 4 x 10 week hours; job sharing; and flexible scheduling to accommodate doctor's appointments, school visits, and other needs. Just let employees go. Don't make them take vacation time to go to the school play or a family emergency.

- Some companies offer the benefit of part-time work during slow times of the year. ConAgra is one of them, letting people leave at noon on Fridays during the summer to get a head start on their weekends. We know people have often checked out anyway, even if they are at their desks on Fridays.

- Free lunch could be served on-site to save employees time, which also encourages socializing among groups that might not work together often.

- On-site services such as childcare or wellness and fitness programs could be offered. Some companies have once-a-month massages or shoe shining. They may have extra staff to run personal errands, such as picking up and delivering dry cleaning or offering grocery delivery to the office.

- You could facilitate carpooling or funding for other transportation options

My favorite flexible strategy is unlimited or increased vacation and holiday time. Zappos made unlimited time off popular. People scratched their heads at first, saying, "Well, that's Zappos. It doesn't apply to us." My personal belief and experience is that it is crazy to be tracking vacation time; and by creating a culture of trust, which you should do in any event, unlimited time off works exceptionally well. Low trust levels, along with old-fashioned thinking, make many companies resistant to this idea.

TalenTrust embraces unlimited vacation, and it has worked brilliantly for the last several years in our company. On average, people take about three weeks every year—probably less than they deserve. I know how hard my team works.

Crazy Good Perks Are Powerful

The traditional mind thinks this way: "I've got a two-week vacation policy and then I give employees more based on tenure, and that's plenty. I can't let them work at home because I can't trust them." Get rid of thoughts like that. The world has changed, and you need to update your thinking. Try experimenting by adding one new perk a year and see if it impacts your engagement and retention or helps you attract the A-players you need to succeed.

As with any competitive factor, it is important that you know how your employee benefits compare with what is happening in the marketplace. There is a trend toward crazy-sounding perks that employees love. Surprising to traditional thinkers is that these

perks benefit employers too by increasing productivity and boosting retention. It must always be understood that company culture is the foundation—the cake, so to speak—with these crazy perks being the icing that people notice in the recruitment process. Together, cake and icing create great cultures for high-performing companies.

Inc. Magazine Lists the Top Ten Things A–Players Want[17]

1. Purpose
2. Clearly defined goals
3. Responsibility
4. Autonomy
5. Flexibility
6. Attention
7. Opportunity for innovation
8. Open-mindedness
9. Transparency
10. Proper compensation

17 Lapowsky, Issie, "10 Things Employees Want the Most," *Inc.,* August 27, 2010, www.inc.com/guides/2010/08/10-things-employees-want.html.

Conduct This SWOT Analysis for A-Players

We have to ask ourselves as company leaders, what do A-players want? How do we make and keep our companies attractive to them?

A-players want a rewarding work experience and an exceptional career path. A SWOT analysis (strengths, weaknesses, opportunities, and threats) as it relates to A-players will help you make certain that your culture is right for them. These are some things to ask:

- **Strengths:** Which of the 10 most wanted are we already doing as well as, or better than, the competition? How can we leverage that? What additional things does our culture offer that would attract top talent, like time off for community volunteering, professional development, or career advancement?

- **Weaknesses:** Which of the ten are we not doing; why or why not? Are they a strategic and realistic fit for our culture? If so, what is stopping us from doing them? What other negative factors, internal or external, affect our culture?

- **Opportunities:** Are our competitors vulnerable in any of these ten areas? How can we explain our culture to candidates? Are there new trends in workplace expectations or lifestyle trends where we can be leading edge? Are we properly informed and organized to take advantage of them?

- **Threats:** What are the risks of not offering the ten most wanted, and have we properly assessed those risks? How many of them do our competitors offer and how do we compare overall?

Be Like Steve Jobs: Seek A-Players and Stay Involved

Steve Jobs got the A-players and kept them. He believed recruiting is hard, and I couldn't agree more. Yet people perceive it as easy. We see companies all the time with pent-up demand—companies that haven't been doing things properly for years and then they find a company like TalenTrust, expecting that we can solve their problem in ninety days. Recruitment is complex, and there are a lot of choices for employees, as well as for companies. My advice is to be patient in recruitment and you will be a winner. Steve Jobs believed that a small team of A-players can run circles around any giant team of B- and C-players. I believe that too.

Not only did Jobs understand that recruiting is hard, but he also believed that it was the most important thing he did—so he never delegated it. Are you delegating your most important function? If so, to whom? You can delegate the process of recruitment but, as CEO, you cannot delegate the hire. It is you who must set the stage for an environment in which people appreciate the work they do and one in which they know they work with people who are as talented as they are. It is also key to make it clear that while each individual is appreciated, the work of the team is bigger than any single individual. By assuming the hiring decision, you are demonstrating how important these factors are and how critical it is that this person fits into the team.

In summary, make it easier for employees to do their jobs and balance their work and home lives with unique and business-appropriate perks that reflect your deeper company culture. The improvements in your company's bottom line will confirm that you made the right choices.

CHAPTER 6

Become Simply Irresistible: Make Your Company the One They Want

E*mployers should do everything within reason to make employees happy. Happy employees refer their friends, creating a continuous pipeline of trusted candidates for growth. Red Frog and its treehouse are a perfect example of how to make "happy" work. Red Frog plans events and parties with the goal of making everything fun for their clients. They succeed by making work as fun as possible for their employees. Fun included creating a treehouse, which takes everybody out of the environment that they're normally in, an office with chairs and desks and computers. The founders always dreamed of a treehouse as kids; as adults, the fun environment helps them brainstorm and do more for their clients—and their employees. That is simply irresistible!*

Red Frog is simply irresistible, but it is also not a company many people have heard of. Zappos, which you have likely heard of, on the other hand, is also a company whose focus is creating happiness. They empower their people to give the best customer service ever imagined. There's a story about a Zappos customer who traveled to Las Vegas but forgot her favorite shoes. She called Zappos, and the agent she spoke with looked online but could not find the shoes. So he left the building and went to every mall in Las Vegas until he found the shoes in her size, color, and style. He wrapped them up and personally delivered them to the customer. The Zappos agent did not have to ask anybody whether he could leave the building or shop because the culture of Zappos is such that you do not have to ask anyone. He did what he believed he should do and, happily, the customer got her shoes. Do you think she will shop with Zappos again? Do you think she tells everyone she knows what a great company Zappos is?

Southwest Airlines is another company that empowers its front lines to create an exceptional customer experience. And what is an exceptional customer experience? It is giving the customer what they want, when they want it, and how they want it within the guidelines of your company. When Southwest CEO Gary Kelly works with a vendor, he has been known to "marry" the vendor during a wedding ceremony. It is symbolic, of course, but it shows his commitment. The "ceremony" is about the companies joining forces. The idea is based on making a commitment to deliver exceptional service to each other—much like in a marriage.

Start Here: Questions for Any Organization

You do not have to be quite as creative as building tree houses or marrying your customers to be irresistible. Although we hear mainly about irresistible tech companies, any organization can become irresistible. The first step is taking a deep, internal reading. Following is a list of questions to ask yourself:

- Do we have culture by default, or do we have culture by design?

- What specific things do we do to ensure our company is a place where people want to come to work, feel valued, and can contribute?

- Does our selection process ensure that candidates fit within our culture?

- Do people work in small teams that can impact real change?

- Are people encouraged to make time to ponder, tinker, and create?

- Do managers help set goals and provide frequent feedback and coaching?

- How much professional and leadership development is offered?

- How meaningful is our performance management system?

- Is our work environment flexible and humane?

- Is there exceptional opportunity for employees to grow?

- How clear have we made our mission and purpose, and are employees inspired by them?

- How high are trust levels between leadership and employees—employees and leadership?

It is a challenge to become irresistible and stay that way as you grow. As the CEO of a small company, you think your company should be run in a certain way, and you surround yourself with like-minded people. Often, these people are friends and family or colleagues you have worked with successfully in the past. The culture is imbedded in how you are together as a small group.

There are big companies that do culture really well and have lots of systems, processes, and people focused on that effort. Some small companies do it well simply because of their size. It is usually in the in-between stages that you experience growing pains. As your company grows, be purposeful about how that growth is reflected in your culture. As you bring on more people, periodically ask the questions above for guidance.

Define Your Core Values, Then Practice Them

Netflix has pages and pages that describe its core values, related to things like judgment and purposefulness and what they mean internally to Netflix. They hire and fire based on their core values, as every company should. At smaller companies, like TalenTrust for example, core values do not typically go on for pages, but whether you are a large organization or small, you need to challenge your core values regularly, making sure they are still relevant to your mission and culture.

At TalenTrust, we challenge our assumptions about our core values in terms of whether we are giving enough definition to them. It is important to clearly define what drives us. In your company, how often do executives evaluate your core values, which are usually just four or five words written on a plaque that hangs in the lobby? How much are executives modeling your values, and are they embedded in your culture? Do people fully understand them, and what kind of behaviors exemplify them? Do people get hired and fired based on these core values?

If you interview and hire based on your core values, it will come naturally to your employees to live them—which puts you well on your way to accomplishing your mission and goals.

It takes courage to begin interviewing for values because you have to first review whether your culture and business practices are aligned with your values and whether your people are living them—or even if they can live them in your current environment. It may mean some uncomfortable analysis and adjustments. Once you have made the decision to be a values-based organization, follow this process:

- Assemble a small, representative group to clearly define your values and communicate them throughout your organization.

- Understand how employees and candidates experience the values. Asking your top performers about their experiences is particularly helpful.

- Incorporate values-based questions into the interview process and train managers in values-based interviewing.

- Articulate and incorporate values-based behaviors into performance expectations and reviews.

It is critical to hire great people, people who are aligned with your values and who live them. After all, it is not your company that creates the personal relationships and emotional bonds with your customers—it is your people. Make interviewing for values your primary employment brand strategy.

A company's culture is one of those things that you cannot put your finger on easily, yet you know it is there. I compare it to being in a family. You don't realize the culture of your family until you go to another and spend time with them. You realize they all sit down and they eat dinner together and yours does not, for example. Perhaps they celebrate birthdays in a certain way, or they encourage certain things among the people in the family, or it is expected that you talk to each other at a meal.

The same thing happens in companies. How do companies reward people? How do companies communicate? Is it all email? Is it tons of meetings? How do companies innovate? How do they engage with clients and engage with each other? Sometimes it is intangible and difficult to describe. For this reason, I advise companies to link back to their core values as a way to say, "This is what we are putting front and center. This is how we're going to behave in support of these core values." For companies that live their values and also have a strong culture, those values are more than just words on a wall or on a website.

Understanding the challenges and triumphs of the people you are interviewing is also important. You have to understand where people are coming from and if they are going to fit your culture. To paraphrase Coach John Wooden, "Character is what you do when no one is watching." This is a component of creating culture by design in your company. It is important to make sure people understand what you stand for so they will know what is expected of them and what they must stand for, whether or not anyone is watching.

You do not define your character by talking about it, whether at a bar or in the office. Other people define your character, and that includes character as a person and character or "brand" as a company. Character in a person can be aligned with the culture in a company. "What do you stand for?" is the question to ask yourself and clearly define.

Hire for Character and Culture First, Competence Second

It is almost an adage in this country that you "hire for competence but fire for character." Although it is true that none of us wants to fly on an airplane built by an apprentice, you can hire an apprentice and teach the necessary mechanical skills. What cannot be taught are the ethics that keep that apprentice from covering up a small crack in the fuselage instead of reporting or repairing it. Whatever else your business has going for it, it won't matter unless you hire people with good character to fulfill your purpose.

There is nothing neutral about character. Employees who do not share your corporate culture dilute it. They detract from the essence that defines your company and drives your achievement. Hiring good cultural matches not only helps to ensure a sustainable future for your business, but it is cost effective—leading to higher retention, better engagement, and deeper relationships with customers. If you find that you have to fire someone for character, damage has already been done.

No one would suggest that a business could succeed without competent employees. What is important to understand is that the long list of "required" competencies companies use as the first phase in screening candidates is the wrong way to go about finding the right people. Look first for the kind of character and culture fit that spawn servant leaders and a sense of community. Then train your people in any skills they lack. No matter what your product or service, you will have the advantage.

Focus on becoming simply irresistible to your employees. Only then can your company become the one that candidates flock to and the one that A-players never want to leave. This takes time and energy, but what results is a loyalty that is absolutely priceless.

CHAPTER 7

Allow for Vulnerability

"It is not the critic who counts, not the man who points out how the strong man stumbles, or where the doer of deeds could have done them better. The credit belongs to the man who is actually in the arena, whose face is marred by dust and sweat and blood, who strives valiantly, who errs, who comes up short again and again, because there is no effort without error and shortcoming, but who does actually strive to do the deeds; who knows great enthusiasms, the devotions; who spends himself in a worthy cause, who at the best knows in the end the triumph of high achievement, and who at the worst, if he (or she) at least fails while daring greatly so that his place shall never be with those cold and timid souls who neither know victory nor defeat."

—Theodore Roosevelt

Theodore Roosevelt might have said this nearly a century ago, but the idea of daring greatly and allowing ourselves to be vulnerable remains relevant today. In fact, it is the topic of a book by speaker and vulnerability expert Brené Brown, who in 2012 penned *Daring Greatly: How the Courage to Be Vulnerable Transforms the Way We Live, Love, Parent, and Lead.* Brown says, "Vulnerability sounds like truth and feels like courage. Truth and courage aren't always comfortable, but they're never weakness ... Vulnerability is the birthplace of love, belonging, joy, courage, empathy, and creativity. It is the source of hope, empathy, accountability, and authenticity." Her words apply equally to organizations and individuals.

In my conversations with companies, I encourage them to explore the role of vulnerability in company cultures. Management teams must have many tough conversations in order to allow themselves to be vulnerable with employees. Otherwise, how can management prepare to lead people through crisis and uncertainty?

When we talk of vulnerability, we are talking about companies getting healthy from the inside out and daring to look at themselves more intimately. It might seem easy when you are in the executive suite, assuming everything is okay because you are looking only at the financials. Are you getting close to your customers, close to your employees, and really understanding what is important to them? When companies look inside themselves, they often find something broken and unhealthy within. They might want quick fixes, but a Band-Aid for an open wound is not enough.

Understand
Big C and Little C

Curt Coffman, coauthor of *First Break All the Rules*, calls Big C the overall organizational culture encompassing its mission, vision, values, strategy, the things hanging on the walls, and all else that is driven by leadership. The other he calls Little C, which is the local culture, driven by individual supervisors and managers and the subcultures within departments or locations. No matter how small you are or how big you are, you as the leader, entrepreneur, CEO, hired gun—or whoever you are—must have a vision of your culture. That's your Big C. That is what you want, your dream. The reality of your culture is the Little C. It is what everybody is doing daily and how they are interacting with each other and your customers.

The Little C is the culture to focus on, looking internally to your company policies and your employees and externally to your customers' experience to identify the real, day-to-day culture, versus your personal vision for culture. Simply put, the "real" culture of an organization is only as big as a single person or a supervisor's domain, which could make an employee's company culture experience the opposite of what the leaders of the organization want it to be. There is a huge amount of power in the Little C. Little C leaders who are aligned with the values and core beliefs of organizations and model the behavior of the overall culture can actually accelerate the company's growth. What does that mean for Little C leaders who are *not* aligned and create a sub-reality for those they touch? You must find the courage to call those people out.

Find the Right People to Fit with You

"You don't hire for skills, you hire for attitude. You can always teach skills. Great companies don't hire skilled people and motivate them; they hire already motivated people and inspire them. People are either motivated or they are not. Unless you give motivated people something to believe in, something bigger than their job to work toward, they will motivate themselves to find a new job and you'll be stuck with whoever's left."

—Simon Sinek

The first step in managing culture is hiring the right people. The right people are aligned with your culture and committed to your values. They have a positive attitude. They are internally motivated. Assessing these qualities in every serious candidate should be an important part of your interview process, yet most companies leave that out. Let's take a deeper look.

Alignment

Since culture defines your employees' work experience, if you hire somebody who is not aligned with your culture, the experience of that employee and the employee sitting next to him or her will affect the performance of both—including their service to your customers. For example, if you were going to hire newspaper journalists or editors, and they were not passionate about storytelling, they would not be a good fit. If they did not want to dig for the truth and just wanted to produce articles and be told what to write, that would not be good alignment for a top newspaper, especially one with an investigative core. The right person for this newspaper would be interested in stories and be innately curious, and because of this, they would be able to relate to colleagues and provide readers with what they want from a dependable news source.

Attitude

Assessing for attitude is another way to ensure cultural fit and is strongly related to the Little C, especially if someone's supervisor has a bad attitude. The attitude of a single employee affects everyone who is near, for better or for worse. Sincere listening and respect are two signs of a positive attitude. When people feel heard and respected, organizations reap the benefits of better retention and job performance, not to mention profits. Listening and empathizing skills are among the most important attributes of effective leaders, from supervisors to the CEO. Part of a leader's job is making people feel good about themselves so that they want to stay with the company and are productive. It can make a huge difference in retention levels whether people *love* working for you or just *like* working for you—and that often depends on the interest leaders take in each of their people.

When leaders do not take an active interest in their employees, the results can be disastrous, spreading out from single supervisor-to-employee relationships to infect teams, departments, and company-wide morale. This is particularly the case with acquisitions, when a company and all of its employees may suddenly be acquired overnight.

Be very careful who you have integrating the new employees into your culture, or your entire investment could vanish.

I experienced the trauma of an acquisition myself when I was working at a larger, traditional staffing company in the early 2000s. We had just acquired a gem of a little company. It had great processes, great people, great brand, and great culture. However, the vice president of the company I was working for was dangerous. She was a person who masqueraded as thoughtful and caring but was truly only focused on her outcomes. I will never forget getting a phone call from her while I was on maternity leave in the fourth quarter of 2000. She was concerned about the integration and high cost of the excellent team we had just acquired. When we acquired the new company, this VP promised in one of our early meetings that we would keep each employee's compensation "whole." Later, she wanted to redefine "whole." I was shocked! Her definition ultimately caused each and every acquired employee to leave us. She and I obviously were not a cultural fit, which brings me to the question: "Why are some people motivated only by their own gain?"

Motivation

Simon Sinek speaks on the "why" that motivates people. Quite often, the answer to "why" has nothing to do with money. It is usually much more complicated than that. These are three key concepts that feed motivation and help explain the "why": recognition, a healthy work environment, and the matter of getting and giving respect.

- **Recognition**. Let's face it—all of us want some kind of recognition. Without it, we don't know whether we are doing the right thing or if anyone even notices or appreciates what we do. Recognition is closely tied to engagement. Recognition can be as simple as saying thank you, although depending on the effort put forth, it is definitely not always enough. Recognition should be appropriate in both timing and method.

- **Environment.** Employees want a healthy work environment, and they want the mission and goals of their company to match their personal goals. Have you asked employees about their personal goals? Where are they trying to go in their careers? What are they trying to achieve for themselves? What are they trying to achieve for their family? Where do they want to be in three to five years? Every manager needs to ask these kinds of questions. The answers might be: "My husband and I want to make sure we have no debt by the time we're thirty-five years old." Or, "I want to make sure I can buy my first home by the time I'm thirty-two." Or, "I want to make sure that I'm on the executive team by the age of forty." Whatever the goals, honor them because they are important to your people.

- **Respect.** Southwest Airlines founder Herb Kelleher used to say that you have to treat your employees right, like they are customers, and then they will, in turn, treat your customers right. In his company, respect has become contagious. As this can work in reverse, every company must have a zero tolerance for a lack of respect among employees and management if you are truly going to run a company of great values. Small things like returning e-mails and phone calls can show respect.

When you find a candidate who is aligned with your values and culture, has a positive attitude, and is motivated to do their best, you know you have the right person. Never jeopardize that by putting them under a supervisor or next to a colleague who is not a fit. Hire the right people throughout your organization.

Build Respect

Respect is the foundation for more than motivation in your company. Trust and morale—those nebulous, hard-to-measure-but-dangerous-to-ignore aspects of your culture—are based on respect. The seeds of respect are found in honest and frequent communication.

Another aspect of respect that is not at all difficult to measure is compensation. I remind companies regularly that the amount of money you pay your people is not just a financial decision; it is also a tangible symbol of how much you respect them. I tell companies to please pay a fair wage. So many companies like to play games with compensation. Make sure you do not put people in the situation where they can't afford to pay their rent or put food on the table. That, too, is a matter of respect. It is important not to get someone on the cheap just because you can. You want to know that your staff is not struggling so your employees can be fully engaged and aligned with the company's mission.

6 Ways to Build Respect with Your Employees

- Set expectations so employees know what they need to do to succeed, and train them so they have the opportunity to succeed.

- Encourage employees to express their ideas and opinions, and then listen and respond, which is almost a more important point, even if that response is "I don't know."

- Require managers to take the time to understand what their people want in addition to wages, and know what is going on in their lives.

- Empower individuals, and do not micromanage.

- Provide opportunities for employees to see the results of their work.

- Recognize and reward individual achievement and behaviors and celebrate often.

Lead with VULNERABILITY in Dynamic Companies

High-growth companies are dynamic but also vulnerable and uncertain. Some people thrive on that uncertainty, finding that it sparks their creative juices. At the same time, it also means management must be aware of and expressive of the vulnerability. We see this in particular with start-ups, especially those that expand very quickly. At the same time, vulnerability can come when a company buys another company or is bought by one. Uncertainty abounds when you are suddenly part of a new company or when the former owner is no longer the company leader after a buyout. Entrepreneurs in particular need to understand this and be straightforward and honest with employees. Good communication will help your current staff and new hires face the level of uncertainty in a changing environment.

How do you charge into the future with the kind of drive and passion that motivates others to follow you when you yourself have no sense for what the future might hold? Today, leaders often do not know what must be done, much less how to go about doing it. But the need for a clear and constant vision is still present and perhaps even more necessary. If you are the leader, you have no choice but to lead change. Be at peace with that and with yourself. Take risks and learn from them.

You Don't Have to Know It All

A component of being vulnerable is admitting that you do not always know what to do. You, as the leader, do not always have all the answers. You, as the leader, are marching forward optimistically, believing in your vision, believing in your dreams, but you really do not know what is around the corner. Having that optimism to charge into the future with such unknowns is quite remarkable, and it takes a unique person to do that.

When advising leaders, I tell them that it is okay to let your people know that you do not know. It is actually empowering to them when you say, "I don't know," because it gives them permission to also not know. And don't forget that there is great power in figuring out what the answers are together, versus telling your people what to do and leading them there. You do not have to put out breadcrumbs for them to follow every step. They can draw their own map to the result, especially if you have hired people with drive and resilience. Lead through your values and your conviction and your optimism. They will provide the direction and resilience you need.

Failing Is an Option

One question leaders in changing environments should ask themselves is, "What would I attempt to do if I knew I would not fail?" Brené Brown has also asked the question in this way, "What's worth doing even if you knew you would fail?" However you phrase it, I like the advice that David Letterman gave to Jerry Seinfeld early in the younger comedian's career. He told him it is okay to fail in what you do, as long as you have the courage to do what you intended and wanted to do. I think both of them have done all right over the years with this advice.

Our challenges today in the business world are remarkable. Over the past decade or so we have had so many things to overcome, including the fear of failure. If you are an entrepreneur, you could fail. It is phenomenally courageous of you to start a business. Give yourself a hand for doing so, and talk about that experience with your employees to let them see how you face your own fears and vulnerability with bravery. As a leader today, you provide vision in the midst of change and chaos. Choose the people who can help you find a likely road to success—any of which will be fraught with challenge.

This goes back to our very first chapter where we talked about letting go of our egos. The concept of being vulnerable is the opposite of leading from ego. With start-ups in particular, we want to believe that everything will be great. It can be, but there is always a sense of vulnerability, especially early on. Don't make it the elephant in the room.

Have Compassion as a Leader

Compassion helps you understand that people have lives outside of your company.

I will share with you a story from TalenTrust. We have somebody in a key position in our company who went through a very trying personal situation because of an ill and dying parent. It happened right after I hired this person. The employee was drawn away from Colorado to be with his family—the right priority. After some time, it finally reached the point where frequent absence and distraction were clearly impacting his work.

Before taking any action, I sat down with some advisers and asked, "What should I do? I have a great deal of compassion for this person." Several people said, "Well, cut the employee loose, fire the person. You know, the person is obviously distracted, and you need somebody to focus on the business." My attorney said, "You have absolutely no obligation to do anything for this person."

Then I sat down with the employee and talked about it. The decision came down to me, and I decided to offer an unpaid personal leave to let this person focus on his family. After ninety days, we would reassess the situation. Sadly, his mother deteriorated and passed away in that time period. The employee returned and is one of the most loyal people I could ever imagine working for my company. I had choices, and I was within my legal right to eliminate the position. Importantly though, I made the right choice based on my moral compass. I had already put a lot of time, energy, and effort into the relationship with this person, so I wanted to see the person through a rough time. Like Robert Frost's road less taken, this has made all the difference.

If you are a CEO, an entrepreneur, or a small business owner reading this book, you have control over how your company treats people. You have the authority to create a respectful environment. You have the ability to buck normal, expected business procedures because it is your company. You have the ability to be brave, to do things differently. You do not have to do things the way everybody else is doing things. Get outside your comfort zone. Get outside the status quo. Get outside the norm and do what matters for your employees and your customers and reflects your ethics.

I guarantee that in doing so, you will be successful.

CHAPTER 8

Be the Tortoise and the Hare

There have been many interpretations of Aesop's fable about the speedy hare versus the slow and steady tortoise, and here's mine: When a person with the right attitude, values, and cultural fit walks in your door, hire him or her with lightning speed and allow all the time he or she needs to learn the necessary skills to succeed in your organization. When you see an employee blaming others, making excuses, or being disrespectful, fire that person with equal speed and take whatever time is necessary to replace him or her with the right person.

Everyone is in a hurry, often for the wrong reasons. No, you do not need to hire someone who isn't a fit because you need the help. And no, you do not need to put up with a bad attitude for even a day. Most of the companies we advise have tried a variety of things by the time they reach out to us—bringing with them a long list of open positions that have gone unfilled for quite a while. One company we have been speaking to recently needs to hire fifteen to twenty people within a six-month time frame. They are already behind the curve because they should have started planning earlier.

Planning is integral to all aspects of managing a company. Think about it. You plan for your revenue. You need to also plan for the people to support your revenue generation. Companies that wait to look for a service provider to address their hiring needs when they are already in emergency mode must realize that a good provider will take the time, energy, and effort for success. A quality recruiter must play tortoise to your hare so that, in the end, you can win. As we have indicated throughout this book, there is a shortage of quality talent, and that talent has choice. Quick hiring miracles are rare and inevitably take more than a simple phone call to a recruiter and a thirty- to sixty-day fix.

When to Be a Tortoise

Jeff Tarr, the CEO of DigitalGlobe, talks about his own values and how he expresses them in his company. Among the things he has said on the topic is, "Our values are about what we do when things get hard. You see people's true colors, as well as your company's, under stress."

Does your company interview and hire for core values? Or do your values show a different color under the stress of needing bodies to get business done when key positions are unfilled? Don't buckle under the stress of empty seats. You'll get long-term value by taking your time to find employees you can count on to live your core values and show your customers who you truly are every day. Short-term employee fixes will also mean short-term customer relationships. In being thoughtful in your hiring, you lead naturally with your values and with bravery in choosing to do the right thing.

There are several values that are or should be hanging on every company's wall and are worth slowing down to consider.

Integrity

Integrity is a soft skill and difficult to define. There are many things you can do to assess someone's integrity, and all candidates should be tested for it. For example, there is a tool from Profiles International called Step One. With a minimal investment, the tool can help you understand if people are inclined to be dishonest or dishonorable in the workplace. It hits at the heart of the concept to hire first for character and culture and second for competencies and skills.

Character

Closely related to integrity is the concept of character. There is nothing neutral about character; people have it or they don't. People with character choose to respond to your company's values by living them. Employees with little character dilute your values and detract from the essence that defines your company and drives your achievement.

Servitude

One of the companies I admire most is WOW! Wide Open West. They have a very simple philosophy of living up to their name. The organization cultivates and nurtures four values, one of which is servitude. WOW!'s former CEO, Colleen Abdoulah, has said, "It means driving genuine satisfaction, taking care of each other and our customers. Hiring authentically people-first employees certainly has much to do with WOW!'s exceptional growth year after year." The company has top rankings on *Consumer Reports* and wins awards every year.

In living the value of servitude, WOW! has created a community of both employee fans and customer fans. This makes great sense. It enables you to understand what is important to your customers and develop your product and service around that. And, equally important, it ensures that you have a culture of employees who are raving fans. These concepts that work so well for WOW! are surprising to many companies.

Most companies we talk with nod their heads, agreeing that hiring based on values and taking time to consider them make sense, yet they are not doing it. It is always interesting to me to find out why. No one would suggest that a business could succeed without competent employees. What is important is to understand that there is a long list of required competencies that you must screen for, but company interviewers are not naturally taking the time to screen for things such as character and integrity.

When to Be a Hare

Be Quick to Fire

Don't delay firing someone by rationalizing that it will be too time consuming and costly to find a replacement. Procrastinating only gives the person who is about ready to depart more time to leave their black marks. If they are not doing quality work, they are no happier than you are. Take action or it will hurt your business—and move quickly.

Many people in business have heard of the halo effect, where our first impression creates a positive bias toward our overall judgment of a person. Sometimes when we interview people, we are so excited about what we *think* they can do that we forget to dig down on what they really *can* do, what their character is, and what their values are. Somebody might walk into your office with all the right credentials, but if you do not take the time to dig down, you may find that the halo effect leads to a bad hire.

Find and Toss the Bad Apples

When people are not working out, there is also the bad apple effect, which means their bad behavior or attitude spreads beyond them to create a toxic atmosphere. The bad apples in your organization, who are not the right fit, are talking to your customers. That should be motivation enough to get rid of them. They are also talking to your A-player employees and bringing them down. They manifest in what I call the "Eeyore Effect." Everyone around them is affected by their lack of energy and their belief that everything is terrible and wrong. If you think of Eeyore, the character from "Winnie the Pooh," what you really need to do is hire Tiggers and Piglets, not Eeyores. What you want are employees who demonstrate energy, not lethargy, and spread it to others. Eeyores are B- and C-players who lower the performance bar. They cause resentment and eventual attrition by A-players, who will move on when they feel they are ignored or when the environment becomes negative.

Statistics support quick action. Leadership IQ tracked twenty thousand new hires and found that 46 percent of them failed out of companies within eighteen months. Interestingly, the researchers found with this failure rate that 89 percent of the time it was for attitudinal reasons and only 11 percent of the time for a lack of skill.[18] The attitudinal deficits that doomed these failed hires included a lack of coachability and low levels of emotional intelligence, motivation, and temperament.

This means it is important to be fast to fire when it clearly is not working out.

We all make mistakes in hiring; they are unavoidable. Face up to the bad hires, and take action. Many times, hiring managers will try to hide their mistake. Instead, as a company leader, you want to create a culture where you can say to employees, yes, you made a mistake, but how quickly are you going to fix it? One mistake will not destroy the company. However, not firing that mistake right away can put a major strain on your entire team.

---

18 Murphy, Mark, "Why New Hires Fail (Emotional Intelligence Vs. Skills)," June 22, 2015, www.leadershipiq. com/blogs/leadershipiq/35354241-why-new-hires-fail-emotional-intelligence-vs-skills

Lots of things can change. Circumstances can change for individuals. Circumstances can change within a company. However, the core values of a person do not change. We must remember what Tarr has said about our values under pressure. Things change in companies all the time. Almost every ninety days, something is changing. How can your people respond to that rapid change during a time of pressure? Those people who cannot keep up are usually the people who must go.

TalenTrust has its own example of a bad hire with a large halo. This employee was one of the best production recruiters I had ever seen, lining up positions, getting candidates to clients, knocking down the contracts, and moving on. However, this person was also mean to others—what I would call an internal "terrorist." He had to go because he was a cancer in our company. Some people include these individuals in the bad-apple category, but at TalenTrust, we call them terrorists. You have to get them out of your organization when they disrespect colleagues and clients. Everybody is watching to see how you handle the terrorist.

Ideally, you are a company that believes culture is king, and you hire and fire based on your values. In spite of this, you might have someone in your organization who does not live by your values. Many companies do the math and decide to keep the person on board because he or she produces significant revenue. Are you going to let that person go based on your values? Those are hard decisions, and if you have a company built on culture and values, those are the choices you have to make. Those criteria apply equally to the janitor and to the CEO, who, by the way, can't hold employees to one standard and operate personally on another.

Ready-to-Go Candidates Are a Solution

Part of being slow and steady is having a pipeline of ready-to-go candidates. It is just as important as having a pipeline of future customers to drive your revenue. We see time and again that companies do not develop a pipeline of applicants for their key positions before the need arises. Instead, companies function in a reactive mode, and they realize too late that change is inevitable in sales or operations or finance or some other area of the company. It might already be ninety days past the initial need by the time they start looking for the right people to replace someone or add to the team.

You can draw on the people who work for you because often the best employees will give you the best referrals for like-minded people, as long as your culture is strong. It is important to make sure foundationally that you have a good company with a good reputation that will pull people in.

It is also important to keep your employees informed. Tell them about the kinds of people and skills you need. Knowing good people ahead of time is key because they might not be in a position to make a move and join your company when you first meet them. In the same way that customers need to be contacted eight to twelve times before they make a buying decision, people who are currently employed with another company need to have eight to twelve contacts before they are going to move from a situation that seems secure to another opportunity. You might reduce that number of contacts if their friend works for you and raves about it.

Cameron Herold's Fire Fast Advice

I have had the pleasure of hearing author Cameron Herold speak twice at Vistage Executive Summits. He is passionate, focused, and objective, with no BS in his style and advice.

One of the most powerful pieces of his presentation is when he talked about a prior employee he had to let go. He was quite emotional about it. When he finally got around to firing this person, the employee asked, "What took you so long? You've been mean and disrespectful to me for so long." Cameron asked his audience, "Does anyone here have someone on their team that they know should go? If so, stand up." Nearly one-third of the five hundred people in the room stood up. Cameron asked us all to go back and set that person free the very next day.

Thankfully, Cameron set his employee free to go and follow his dreams and make his mark in the world. We often have to make these hard decisions and realize that we may be doing these employees a favor by setting them free to do great things of their own choosing. In the process, we allow our own companies to thrive.

Hire When the Opportunity Strikes

On the opposite end, sometimes you must also be opportunistic. On occasion, you meet people who are potential game changers, those who can really impact your company. Do not be pennywise and pound foolish. Make sure you evaluate how and why you can bring them into the company. Do not make hiring decisions based on an annual compensation. Make hiring decisions based on a monthly compensation because things change that rapidly.

Do not fear the annual salary. Just ensure that the person is productive. It is all about the value alignment with the candidate and not just putting butts in seats. It is about being more strategic and thoughtful.

Help your company grow as it needs to, in a race forward where you are both the tortoise and the hare at every turn and with every challenge.

CHAPTER 9

Highlight Your Employment Brand

*T*he hiring manager doesn't understand what people think of the company and why its reputation keeps people from working there. He or she isn't able to get the best candidates to fill open positions. The company's bottom line shrinks, candidates often don't bother to call back, and the hiring manager is left bewildered and challenged by perpetual failure. I've seen it many times.

What is your reputation as an employer? This becomes your employment brand. It is how your employees describe the experience of working for your organization. A strong employment brand clearly communicates the culture of your company, its mission, and its values, giving people a compelling reason to want to work for—and stay with—your organization.

Be Authentic and Strategic

In short, your employment brand—whether it is positive, negative, or nonexistent—significantly impacts your ability to hire top talent. Assessing, improving, and then promoting your employment brand should be a top priority for your organization. Your employment brand is a strategic talent management endeavor that goes well beyond recruitment and must align with your business strategy. It is a long-term effort that permeates every aspect of the employee lifecycle, including recruitment, onboarding, retention, and engagement.

At TalenTrust, we advise companies to evaluate, enhance, and leverage their employment brands in order to compete this candidate-driven market. We also help these companies understand that their employment brand cannot be created; it can only be revealed. The biggest mistake that companies make is trying to manufacture a reputation that doesn't exist or even line up with an accurate experience. That just won't fly in this age of hyper transparency.

Instead, your employment brand must be based on authenticity, a solid business model, and a mission that employees want to support. Your employment brand is just as important as your corporate brand, and it should be aligned with your company's character. Your internal organization and your external brand are no longer two separate entities. It is impossible to separate employees from the brand of your organization because they are a defining part of your brand.

Consider dividing your employment branding strategy into three steps.

- Evaluate: Ask your employees how they experience your company. Would they recommend employment there to their peers?

- Enhance: Listen to the feedback, and identify ways to improve the employee experience.

- Leverage: Develop a messaging platform to describe the employment experience, and use it in recruitment efforts, including employee referrals and recognition as an "employer of choice".

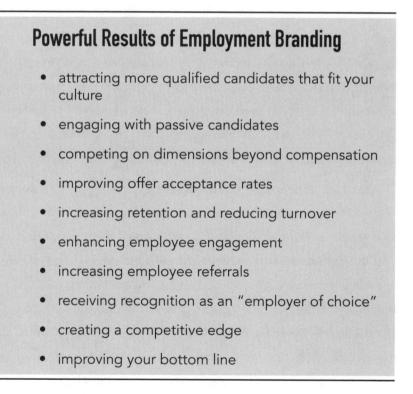

Powerful Results of Employment Branding

- attracting more qualified candidates that fit your culture

- engaging with passive candidates

- competing on dimensions beyond compensation

- improving offer acceptance rates

- increasing retention and reducing turnover

- enhancing employee engagement

- increasing employee referrals

- receiving recognition as an "employer of choice"

- creating a competitive edge

- improving your bottom line

When you are unable to attract good people, take it as a clear sign that something is wrong—and it is probably a lack of employee engagement. Nothing impacts your employment brand more than a company staffed with dissatisfied or downright unhappy people. But you can change that, and in this chapter we discuss some of the most important elements of engagement that affect your employment brand.

Start with Self-Assessment

We use the Net Promoter Score® at TalenTrust. Introduced by Fred Reichheld in a 2003 *Harvard Business Review* article, it measures the loyalty of customer relationships, calculated based on responses to the question: "How likely are you to refer our firm to a colleague or friend?" The score is assessed on a scale of zero to ten; then the percentage of participants who rate you zero to six (detractors) is subtracted from the percentage who rate you nine or ten (promoters).

Are you brave enough to ask a similar question of your employees? "How likely are you to recommend employment at this company to a friend or family member?" The answer to this question is an important measure of how engaged your employees are.[19] If you do not receive ratings of nine or ten, then you have work to do. If your staff is not willing to refer people they know into the company, they are not happy at work. A lower score should lead to an immediate process of reflection and exploration. Employment brand and employee engagement are almost synonymous. If you have an engagement or retention problem, then you also have an employment brand problem.

---

19 Reichheld, Frederick F. "The One Number You Need to Grow," *Harvard Business Review,* December 2010. https://hbr.org/2003/12/the-one-number-you-need-to-grow.

A case in point is a company we were helping with employment branding at a time they were losing key employees to a competitor. They wanted to understand why people were leaving. This particular company was experiencing high growth as a $65 million office furniture sales company. They are very proud of their sales culture, with its high-urgency, Nordstrom's-level service. They now make it clear to prospective employees that if their culture is not a fit for them, then they should look elsewhere. To hold strong beliefs like these, you must know who you are and why you do what you do as a company, as well as what you are willing to change.

This is a sales company in essence, and that component is not going to change. From their internal analysis, they discovered a few other important things about their organization, some of which they planned to transform. When you look at yourself closely, you must be willing to look at key findings and decide what is vital to your core competencies and culture and what you are not willing to change. By the same token, you must also understand what is not key to your core values and what you are willing to change. In this instance, the company learned that they had to manage their brand by letting others know their values.

A self-assessment is like Michael Jackson's song "Man in the Mirror." You have to look internally, and some companies are afraid to do that. You must ask questions such as: "How do people from outside see our company, and depending on the answer, how do we leverage that employment brand to get great candidates? Did we make the 'Best Places to Work' list in our city, region, or country? If not, why?"

And you need to look honestly and deeply at the answers. The goal is to ensure that your culture focuses on employee engagement, because employee engagement means people are actually having fun doing the work. They want to come to work every day, they are clear about your purpose, and their goals are aligned with your company goals.

Company Size Is No Excuse

Make your company an easy place to work. People want to be productive. Do not make it hard for them. Do not make it hard for people to be successful in your organization.

Everybody knows that people love to work at Facebook, Apple, Google, and Zappos. They are big companies that are household names and spend a great deal of time, money, and creativity attracting and retaining talent. What about the smaller companies that are also doing great work around culture and employee engagement? There are many, and I offer two examples so that you can see how they present themselves to the world on their websites and perhaps find some useful ideas.

- Clockwork in Minneapolis is a well-rated, woman-owned business, with a great management team that maintains fantastic relationships with their employees. They have received several "Best Places to Work" awards.

- One of our Denver clients, LINX, was named a 2015 "Best Places to Work" finalist by the *Denver Business Journal* because their employees love working there. They know that management cares about them and their individual forward momentum in the company.

Many small to midsized companies, like the ones mentioned above, do indeed take time to self-assess to learn more about engagement, and they are better for it. I have to mention one other Colorado company that is excellent at this: New Belgium Brewing. I heard CEO Kim Jordan speak in 2011, and she talked about love in the workplace. Of course, love and acts of kindness and compassion happen in workplaces everywhere but simply not often enough. Why do we hesitate to talk about love in the workplace and going above and beyond and taking care of people?

One example of New Belgium's compassion and love in the workplace is the eternal and universal need to attend funerals. At New Belgium, time off for funerals can be as long as three weeks, instead of the usual two or three days when everything is a blur. This can mean a huge difference in being with one's family before and after a loved one's passing. This deep support during what is truly an awful time can anchor an employee's loyalty to you and your company.

It is crazy that people have to use their days off to go to a funeral. If you still have a dated policy on vacation and PTO time that requires people to use vacation or other paid time off to attend a funeral, you are way behind the times. Do you think people really want to leave work to go to a funeral? Or are you just so suspicious that you think people are lying to you and saying they want to go to a funeral? If that is how your company works, it is past time to reassess. People first—always.

One other note, you cannot be regarded as a great place to work, one that puts people first, if you do not also have good clients. We had a potential client that we decided was not a good fit for us, and we chose not to work with them. One clue was learning that their turnover rate was 330 percent. When we asked the CEO, "What are you going to do about the turnover numbers?" his answer was, "We don't care." My staff and I couldn't get out of the room fast enough. In another example, a TalenTrust client had stopped treating my team with dignity and respect—one of our core values—so we determined it was no longer a good fit. It is important that your employees are serving clients whose values are aligned with those of your company. Otherwise you create dissonance.

Aim for Killer Strategy and Great People

Choose your people carefully. If you are surrounded by people who gossip incessantly and are always gloomy, would you look forward to seeing them every day? Wouldn't it affect your productivity? You must focus on putting your people and your culture first.

I had the pleasure of hearing GolfTEC cofounder Joe Assell speak. He was told repeatedly that his business model would fail. He thankfully ignored the naysayers and took his love of golf to now employ 650 people and earn $80 million in sales. He focuses on having the right people on board, which means not only those with the talent to meet challenges but also people he loves to be around. It is a crazy thought, right? You should choose people that you want to be around. After all, you are going to be around them for a long time each day. And chances are that if you enjoy your people, then they will enjoy each other because you share the same values, right?

Though they should, company leaders do not always choose people based on those they want to spend time with. It goes back to choosing Tigger or Eeyore. Do you want to hang out with a bunch of morose Eeyores, or do you want to hang out with a bunch of upbeat Tiggers? Of course, depending on where you are based and who you are as a company, in some cultures some Eeyore qualities may be the best fit. Still, you must at least be aware that you are hiring an Eeyore or a Tigger—and hiring for the right reasons.

Honor Is the Rock of Engagement

Honor is another concept I believe in very strongly but is also a hard-to-grasp intangible. Honor is an old-fashioned concept. It means integrity in your beliefs and values. You rarely hear it in the workforce today. Usually you hear it when we are referring to the military or more traditional organizations. We need to focus more on honor in business and measure aspects of business around honor in product development, marketing, accounting, distribution—and employment brand. As a company leader, you need to know what your people honor in order to make good hiring decisions that foster engagement.

When I use the word "honorable" to describe someone, I am referring to people who strive to drive out mediocrity within the workplace. They understand the purpose of the company. They understand the mission they are on. They understand where they are going. They focus on the tactics they need to get to the desired outcome. At its essence, honor is about trust and commitment. When you think about it from a military perspective, people in the military follow higher-ranking officials because they trust them. When you put trust in your workplace, you are re-instilling honor.

Because my work centers on people in organizations, I have a deep respect for the role trust plays as the foundation for employee and customer relationships. (I felt the need to honor its importance by making it part of our company name, TalenTrust.) I know that companies are built through the strength of the trust of their people. And I know that employee engagement can only be built on cultures that honor trust.

Recognition Nurtures Employees and Profits

When you recognize that your people have personal lives, you are not only showing your appreciation of them, but you are likely increasing your profitability as an added benefit. This is because when you value them as human beings rather than as "workers," you develop more loyal employees who will gladly do more for the company and its customers. How employees experience you is how your culture and employee brand are actually formed.

Part of recognizing employees is remembering to actually express the basic "please" and "thank you" that are so often taken for granted in organizations. But recognition goes far beyond that to your official polices on how you treat people.

To go back to our earlier funeral example, would you like to be the manager who says, "No, you can't go to your uncle's funeral because we have a deadline to meet"? Your employees understand customer deadlines. Rather than hassling employees in their time of grief, if you recognize that they need to leave without question, you will find that a more dedicated employee returns after the funeral and works until midnight to meet the customer deadline—without being asked. This is an example of how putting people first leads to increased profits and higher levels of satisfaction for you and the employee. What are your policies around attending funerals?

Another major area where you can show recognition is in the caregiving duties that people need to perform, which are often handled in a way that creates great stress for employees. Examining and humanizing your policies on sharing and balancing paternity/maternity leave, along with reentry and transition back into work functions, can actually increase productivity as well as retention of valuable employees.

As an example, when our VP of marketing and sales here at TalenTrust had a baby, she took eleven weeks of leave. She needed to return after her leave as a new mom, with time to see how it was going to work with all the new challenges of balancing work and parenting. In many ways, it is an experiment, and she cannot know until she goes through it just how it will all fit with her schedule both at work and home.

If I, as her boss, had demanded that she immediately begin working from eight to five or seven to six, it would put undue pressure on her. As a company, we are not a punch-the-clock culture anyway. But I have seen many companies that have strict policies about work hours when in reality it makes no difference at all. It is "just the way we've always done things," they say. Our "get the work done; you're an adult, we trust you to do it" culture has made the journey so much easier for our employee to assimilate back into working with this new little person who is fully dependent upon her.

Having or adopting a child is a big deal, for both parents. If you have a maternity leave and not a paternity leave policy, you had better address that immediately. Why is the mother more important than the father during this major life change? Just make the policy open to both and be as generous and full of individual choice as possible. Your policies should reflect honor and trust, which you will get back tenfold.

It is not just new parents who need your recognition and humane policies. Employees may find themselves helping to support more than one generation of family members. Work and life are becoming more fluid. We are available 24/7, 365 days a year. We have smartphones, computers and iPads, and all kinds of other devices. It is nearly impossible these days not to be working evenings and during the weekend. Yet it is important to remember that your employees have responsibilities beyond your company, and their personal time must be respected.

Many of your employees have children, significant others, or aging parents who need them to be accessible. As for myself, my parents are in their eighties and nineties. I live in Colorado, and they live on the East Coast, and if something goes wrong, I am getting on a plane. I can be accessible while I am in Hartford Hospital taking care of whatever I need to do. I can serve anybody all over the country, so you have to trust in me that while I am taking care of my parents, I will take care of my responsibilities to the company. It is a matter of trust that people understand what needs to get done, but in turn, you respect them and trust they will do the right thing.

Of course, some people will not do the right thing. Those who do not, you must invite to leave. But do not start with suspicion. Start with trust. You will get better results.

Roll Out the Welcome Mat

Welcoming new employees into your company after the candidate interview process is itself a special period. I tell companies to roll out the welcome mat or expect a revolving door. This is not catch and release. We want new employees to feel welcome, and we want them to stay.

An effective orientation process begins with how you describe it. Think and talk about it as a welcoming orientation versus an onboarding. Who wants to be "onboarded"?

Why do some companies put enormous amounts of time and energy into hiring and then forget about the next critical step of welcoming new hires and making the most of their first ninety days? Doing seemingly small but thoughtful things can make people feel valued immediately. Send new employees your favorite business-related book and write in the inside cover, "We hope you're with us for the journey." Send them a little note, "We're glad you chose us." Recognize that they choose you as well as you choosing them. And, a tip, don't ask your admin to write the notes; write them yourself, and if you can, drop by and hand them to the new hire personally. If you are the CEO, that creates a powerful sense of belonging. I don't care what size your company is, everybody should at least meet the CEO.

Orientation needs to go well beyond a basic explanation of employee benefits. Far too often, an HR representative rushes through the benefits and then says, "Go off and be successful." There are many great outcomes to a well-thought-out orientation that covers every-thing an employee needs to know to make a positive start, including clear and consistent expectations. Cost savings, better retention, and higher engagement are just three of them.

Give an Effective Orientation

Take the time to lay out everything that is important to a new hire; give people a high comfort level. At a minimum, your welcome should include the following:

First day:

- benefits explanation

- a tour

- introductions to appropriate people

- email address, telephone access, desk, and a computer (tested before arrival)

- an invitation to lunch

First week:

- explanation of products and services and your customer service philosophy

- company history and culture

- expectations

- further introductions

- business cards (the earlier the better—makes people feel immediately part of your team)

In the first thirty days, new employees should not be expected to produce. They should be expected to learn, so it is very important that you give them time to listen, ask questions, and understand. In planning your orientation program, think of your own first day on a new job or your first day of school. You didn't know anyone. You felt ill at ease. You were nervous. You were worried you might make a mistake. You didn't even know where the bathroom was. Orientation is not a one-day event. It should be at least a monthlong process with regular check-backs after thirty, sixty, and ninety days. When you train people, they are only going to absorb a certain amount of the information, and it is important to make sure there is true understanding and retention.

Go beyond the basics. Do not just show them where the bathroom is. Make sure you talk about culture and values and how important they are to your company. Those companies that really focus on culture and value are the winners, as we have been saying throughout this book. Sending welcome packets that might include descriptions of culture and values as well as the company history before the first day on the job can increase the sense of belonging. Arranging a lunch with the CEO and/or other senior team members during that first week is also part of a special welcome.

Make it memorable during that first week and through that first month. You want to increase the comfort level and productivity of new employees. You cannot afford not to. You do not want turnover, and you do not want people who are not aligned to your values coming on board. When you put them through this welcoming phase, if anyone is going to fail, you will see it in the first thirty days if you carefully invest the time. Making the person feel connected to the company helps both of you. Face it, while we know that many people are jazzed by chaos and change, it can still make all of us a little bit nervous.

The goal is to make people comfortable and connected as early as possible. One thing we do to accomplish that goal at TalenTrust is to welcome new employees with a happy hour that follows our monthly team meeting. I should be clear that our happy hours are not mandatory. There is nothing happy about mandatory. After all, you cannot mandate fun, and we also want to be respectful of the after-work time employees are giving to us. We say, "Hey, after our team meeting, let's have a happy hour to welcome our new members and celebrate our team-wide successes. Come if you can." This allows us to learn more about our new people on a more personal level and start building relationships and connections that can be meaningful as people begin working together. (And, by the way, the percentage of people who attend these kinds of optional events can give you additional insight into your engagement level.)

Make everyone feel welcome early on by rolling out the welcome mat, and you will build brand and employee loyalty.

Your reputation as an employer—good, bad, or bland—is now front and center. You will learn a lot when you take the time to understand how current and prospective employees experience your company. After you have sat in their cubicles and walked to the water cooler in their shoes, use this new perspective to evaluate and authentically enhance your company's reputation. In the end, all you have is your reputation, so make sure it is excellent.

CHAPTER 10

Lean In with Lipstick

"Pretty women wonder where my secret lies.
I'm not cute or built to suit a fashion model's size
But when I start to tell them,
They think I'm telling lies.
I say,
It's in the reach of my arms,
The span of my hips,
The stride of my step,
The curl of my lips.
I'm a woman
Phenomenally.
Phenomenal woman,
That's me."

—from "Phenomenal Woman," Maya Angelou

When Maya Angelou explains it, it is poetry. When analysts explain the gender issue, it is hard-fact science. Either way, women rock, and you are a fool if you do not have more women in your company and among your leadership. Our ability to multitask and get things done, along with our level of service, is amazing.

Much of what is included in this chapter applies to both men and women who want to achieve a satisfying work-life balance. Still, high-performing companies recognize and appreciate our differences and the tremendous business benefits of a diverse leadership team.

The Business Reasons for Both Sexes Leading Together

- Companies with more female executives and directors perform better.[20]

- Women leaders are more assertive and persuasive, more willing to take risks, and more able to bring people around to their point of view because they have stronger interpersonal skills.[21]

Companies with a mix of male and female leaders, with their differing attitudes regarding risk, collaboration, and ambiguity, will outperform a competitor that relies on the leadership of a single sex.[22]

20 McKinsey & Company, "Women Matter," Accessed on September 22, 2015, www.mckinsey.com/features/women_matter.

21 Lowen, Linda, "Qualities of Women Leaders: The Unique Leadership Characteristics of Women," About.com Guide, Accessed on September 22, 2015, http://womensissues.about.com/od/intheworkplace/a/WomenLeaders.htm.

22 *USA Today*, "Women CEOs Slowly Gain on Corporate America," ABC News, January 1, 2009, http://abcnews.go.com/Business/CEOProfiles/story?id=6563039&page=1.

When more women are on board, companies tend to be more profitable.[23]

Pick the School Play or the Client Meeting

So many women and men, though mostly women it seems, must choose between going to the school play or to an important meeting at work. How often do employees slink out and take a sick child or ailing mother to a doctor's appointment? It is often difficult to live our core values at work, though it should not be.

I once had the honor of hearing Shelly Lazarus, the former CEO and now chairperson emeritus of Ogilvy & Mather, share her perspective about women in leadership and whether we should go to the school play or the meeting. Her position is among the highest for a woman to have ever achieved in the business world in this country. Lazarus ran Ogilvy & Mather, a top-ten marketing communications firm with more than 18,000 employees and 450 offices in 120 countries. She has been with the organization for forty years. Her model and mentor was company founder David Ogilvy, who initiated her tenure as CEO with these words, "You can never spend too much time thinking about, worrying about, caring about your people, because at the end of the day, it's only the people who matter, nothing else."

In speaking on this topic, Lazarus offered several key takeaways that I have thought much about. One of the most striking: with three children herself, she cautioned that next month you will not

---

23 Allen, Jane, "Women on Boards: Why Would You Do It?" CEO Forum Group, Accessed on September 22 2015, www.ceoforum.com.au/article-detail.cfm?cid=6308&t=/Jane-Allen-Egon-Zehnder-International/Women-on-Boards-Why-would-you-do-it.

remember who was and was not at a meeting, but her son would always remember if she was not at his field day. Other gems:

- You do not need to sacrifice your life for your career.

- Make yourself indispensable and then ask for what you need.

- Do not be afraid to define your priorities and voice them.

- Fear is a good thing. Be brave.

- Figure out your own solutions and purpose.

- You know the right thing to do. Do not wait. Act.

- Do something you love. That is the key to a balanced life.

- Make the most of your opportunities, and accept that you cannot do it all perfectly, in spite of what movies and news media tell us as women in the workforce.

She suggested in her conversation, "Think of everything in terms of outcomes. The outcome of not going to the meeting versus the outcome of not going to the school play." What a great way to ensure that your values are the foundation for every choice you make. Personally, I am going to pick the school play.

Men and Women: Lean In and Lead Together

There are many statistics on women in the workforce. According to McKinsey & Company, companies with more female executives and directors perform better.[24] And Pepperdine finds that women tend to be more assertive and persuasive and more willing to take risks.[25] Companies with a mix of male and female leaders with differing attitudes regarding risk will outperform a competitor that relies on a single sex leadership, according to Rosener.[26]

It is not about women only in leadership. It is about men and women leading together. In this competitive global economy, it is critical that we learn to work together. I hear often from women that they will opt out of a situation if it is predominately male. Why are they opting out? They need to opt in and figure out how to work with men. And men need to value and support women.

I serve on a board of a growing IT contract staffing firm. I am the only woman on the board of advisors. Now, I could decide not to participate because I am the only female. But why would I? Is it scary to be in a room of only men when you offer the only female perspective? Sure, but you can embrace it and flip it on its head by saying to yourself, "Hey, I have a responsibility as the only woman in the room." It is human nature to be somewhat uncomfortable when looking around a room and seeing that, "There's nobody like me here." In my view, with leadership comes the obligation to build relationships with the people in the room who are not like you. More women need to take a leadership position by opting in rather than opting out.

Sheryl Sandberg, the COO of Facebook, wrote the acclaimed book *Lean In*, about women in executive leadership. I think this phrasing

---

24 McKinsey & Company, "Women Matter," Accessed on September 22, 2015, www.mckinsey.com/features/women_matter.
25 Lowen, Linda, "Qualities of Women Leaders: The Unique Leadership Characteristics of Women," About.com Guide, Accessed on September 22, 2015, http://womensissues.about.com/od/intheworkplace/a/WomenLeaders.htm.
26 USA Today, "Women CEOs Slowly Gain on Corporate America," ABC News, January 1, 2009, http://abcnews.go.com/Business/CEOProfiles/story?id=6563039&page=1.

is important, but I also like to use the term "opting in," or "getting in the game." You must be at the table to have your voice heard.

Catalyst.org recently found that fewer than 5 percent of S&P 500 companies have a female CEO, and only 19 percent of companies' board seats are held by women.[27] Conversely, as a side note, as a nation we have this problem when women try to run for the highest positions in our country, particularly Hillary Clinton and Sarah Palin: we focus on their hairdos and clothing. In my experience, this focus too often crosses into the business realm. The focus on leaders should always be on their opinions and actions, guidance, and innovations. While clothing should not be the work focus, women should feel that it is perfectly okay to be authentically feminine in the workplace.

Women Need to Help Other Women

What skills are necessary for women to empower other women, and how can women support each other in the workplace? Aside from mentoring, the first thing that comes to my mind is understanding parenting. To that point, the US Census Bureau predicts that 80 percent of women younger than forty-four in the workplace will be mothers at some point in their careers. For this reason, it is of paramount importance that women do not denigrate other women who choose to become mothers. At the end of the day, give a sister a break. Help another woman succeed. It will make you feel good, and it is the right thing to do.

There is a general notion that women in the workplace undermine one another. There is this little turf war that tends to go on—at least it is something that I have certainly experienced in my career, as have

27 Catlyst.org, "Women in S&P 500 Companies," 2015, www.catalyst.org/knowledge/women-sp-500-companies.

many others. The "queen bee" attitude is that, "It took me a long time to get to where I am. Nobody is going to move me off my perch, definitely not another woman." As women in the workforce, we must stop competing with one another and start embracing one another and our differences as well as our unique contributions. When we begin to promote women in the workplace, we must set in place an environment in which they can succeed.

PowerToFly president Katharine Zaleski wrote an apology to working mothers that appeared in *Fortune* magazine in March 2015.[28] Until she had her own child and knew how much time and effort it took to raise a family and at the same time be a professional, she did not realize how horrible she had been to other women. Prior to this, she had judged other women harshly. At one point, she made a decision that if they were mothers and could not go to the five o'clock cocktails because they had to pick a child up at daycare, they were not worth her time.

After having a child, Zaleski started her company, PowerToFly, which empowers women to work from home so they can be a full person. Quite simply, it is good that so many working women are going to be moms. We want our population to grow. We also want the brainpower of women in the workplace. Zaleski's company is revolutionizing how you can engage women differently and allow them to work from home.

Female employees who work from home are more productive because they do not have to choose. Of course, the same increases in productivity occur when men work from home to care for their family, on average from 13 to 22 percent—along with cost savings on office space.[29]

---

28 Zaleski, Katherine, "Female Company President: "I'm Sorry to All the Mothers I Work With," Fortune, March 3, 2015, http://fortune.com/2015/03/03/female-company-president-im-sorry-to-all-the-mothers-i-used-to-work-with/.
29 Boyer O'Leary, Michael, "Telecommuting Can Boost Productivity and Job Performance," *U.S. News*, March 15, 2013, www.usnews.com/opinion/articles/2013/03/15/telecommuting-can-boost-productivity-and-job-performance.

Lessons from *Lean In*

"We stand on the shoulders of the women who came before us, women who had to fight for the rights that we now take for granted," writes Sheryl Sandberg.

Sandberg offers plenty of statistics to support this fact that men still run the world. Example: "Of 197 heads of state, only twenty-two are women." Another fact: of the top five hundred companies by revenues, only twenty-one are headed by women. In politics, women hold just 18 percent of congressional offices.

And she covers women's compensation. Though it used to be worse—in 1970, American women made fifty-nine cents for every dollar men earned—it is still bad. In 2010, women earned just seventy-seven cents for every dollar men made. Her solution: negotiate like a man.

Sandberg writes extensively about the barriers women still face in the workplace, including "blatant and subtle sexism, discrimination, and sexual harassment." She underlines the importance of workplace flexibility and the need for accessible childcare and parental leave policies. She also notes a 2011 McKinsey study showing that while men are promoted based on potential, women get a leg-up based on past accomplishments.

She also argues convincingly that internal obstacles hold women back. "We lower our own expectations of what we can achieve," she writes. She says that women keep themselves from advancing because they do not have the self-confidence and drive that men do.

Mentoring Other Women Is Right, Rewarding, and Too Rare

"Mentor and coach others whenever you can. Your teaching will deepen your own learning."

—Lee J. Colan

If you are a woman in business, when was the last time you mentored another woman or helped another woman move forward in her career? We must mentor other women because we are still a minority in many areas of business, despite being just over half of the population. For instance, fewer than 2 percent of women-owned businesses ever achieve one million in revenue or greater. It is true that a lot of the entrepreneurial smaller companies under one million are founded by women, but rarely do they reach more than one million in revenue. This is an astounding statistic, but we can do something about it, working together.

I have mentored young women over the years. Right now, I am mentoring a woman whose mother died from ALS, Lou Gehrig's disease. She had to take care of her mom for two years, and that created what is usually seen as a negative hole in her resume. She has re-entered the workforce and did not have a female counterpart to help her do that. A client introduced me to her. I have absolutely nothing to gain other than giving a hand back to this bright, amazing, capable young woman in her twenties. In many ways, she reminds me of who I was twenty-five years ago, and I want to help her on her journey.

The Mentors in My Life

From personal experience, I can say that a mentor is like nothing else in your life. If you do not have one, find one. If you have already arrived, I hope you will become one. Mentors guide us to a new destination in life, and sometimes we don't even know where that is. They teach us to be the best at what we are to become.

Mentors have walked the path before you and have been to the places you are headed. They offer you life and leadership skills, vision and perspective, wisdom and feedback. They present new experiences and connections and a place to test your ideas. They lift your performance, increase your confidence, and provide opportunity. Perhaps most important, mentors have already failed and can make sure that you do not. They ask the right questions and help you identify risks and avoid land mines.

If you ask successful people how they got there, inevitably they mention at least one important mentoring relationship somewhere along the way. Actually, it is hard for me to imagine how anyone can be their best without the guidance of a mentor. Some of my richest relationships have been with mentors. I have been very lucky …

My first mentor was my father. Because he believed in me, I believed in myself. Dad instilled my values and gave me confidence. His early and ongoing mentoring has made me a better person overall—and a better wife, mother, and friend. He is in large part why I became me.

I met another important life mentor, David Mead, in the late 1990s. For no other reason than he saw a spark in me, a young woman trying to succeed, he began to open doors in my professional life. He introduced me to the Association for Corporate Growth (ACG) and to a world I barely knew existed—the world of venture capitalists, investment bankers, and deal making. Over fifteen years, Dave guided and advised me as I became an ACG board member and then president of the board, and I have grown my business to heights I may not have contemplated without his mentoring. I thank Dave most for expanding my vision.

Mentoring relationships develop and nurture you into the next best version of yourself—whatever that might be. I believe strongly that people are working toward a better self, and mentors are the guides to get us there. If you want to reach the highest peaks, you hire a Sherpa to guide you. If you want to be a leader, you need a mentor.

I have had many mentors in addition to my dad and Dave, and I, myself, am now a mentor. I get particular satisfaction in mentoring young women much like myself of not too many years ago. One of my mentees recently became the thirty-something CEO of a $40 million company. And am I proud of her. Mentoring is an immensely gratifying way to help someone else succeed and to thank your own mentors by paying it forward.

The great thing about mentoring relationships is that they do not need to follow the traditional elder-junior model. They can be with anyone, anywhere. You can find a mentor or be a mentor in peer-to-peer relationships, across functions or industries, and in personal or professional situations—former or informal. Mentoring is about filling skill or knowledge gaps, sharing, and growing.

Mentoring relationships are about caring enough to invest your time in another person, whether you are teaching or learning, so that you both successfully reach your destination—wherever it turns out to be.

Since we need more women leaders, if you are a woman, mentor another woman. If you are a man, mentor a woman. You will be creating better business.

"The greatest good you can do for others is not just to share your riches but to reveal to them their own."

—Benjamin Disraeli

CHAPTER 11

Empathize with Hourly Employees

❝ *My employees will leave me for twenty-five cents,"* the manager said as he toured his factory. *"If it is fifty cents, if it's twenty-five cents, just give it to them. It costs more not to."*

It costs so much more to replace somebody than to pay that person a little more. Do the math. What is the cost of retention or replacement? (Figure *all* of your costs: lower productivity; over-worked, stressed remaining staff; lost knowledge; retraining costs; internal recruiting time or external fees; potential loss of customers; etc.) Every time, retention wins.

Everyone is important at every level in your company—blue collar, white collar, purple collar, orange collar, it doesn't matter. Everybody has a role in the success of the company. I think sometimes there is a negative connotation to the term "blue collar"—that these workers are less important. Imagine manufacturing a product without them! Everyone deserves respect no matter what the role.

Management is often disconnected from the lives of their hourly workers, especially the C-suite. Think about yourself—when was the last time you had to worry about buying bread and salami versus just buying the bread? Far too often, people who make salaried incomes, especially in the high figures, are removed from the reality of someone trying to provide for a family with wages of twelve or fifteen dollars an hour. Typically, those of us in the executive level don't even think about that anymore.

In reality, fifteen dollars an hour is only $31,200 annual income, gross. How terrible that people have to decide whether to feed their family just bread, or bread and salami, much less choosing whether to eat at all or pay for medical care. When you think about your hourly workers, how much stress is in their lives just to survive? If we can remove that as employers, how much more loyal and engaged will those people be in our workforce?

If you have hourly employees, be fair with their pay rates because it benefits your people and your company. In Los Angeles, New York, San Francisco, and other cities, fair wages are currently in the news as new legislation is considered. Remember that even your hourly people can be wooed away. Give them what they need, and pay them at least 25 percent more than your competitors.

I have met CEOs who hated to part with an extra twenty-five cents per hour for employees. A quarter. It might not seem like much of a difference to a CEO making a six-figure salary, but twenty-five cents is important to people at the bottom of the pay scale. Stop holding them hostage for it. They are trying to feed their families. If an hourly-waged employee goes across the street for twenty-five cents, guess what? They may take four or five of their friends with them.

Eliminate the executive disconnect, and try to get inside your employees' minds with empathy. Get in the mind of your customers as well—and I argue that your employees are also your customers. How you treat them has a direct impact on how they treat your paying customers. In some ways, this was the Ford model of the automotive industry: pay your employees well enough that they can afford to buy your products. It makes perfect sense to me.

Consider Who Does the Heavy Lifting

It is important to remember that it is your entry-level employees who are doing the heavy lifting, the day-to-day operations that are critical to making your business vision a reality. You can create the greatest product in the world, but if there is no one to put it on a truck, how can you get it to your customers?

If turnover has increased by 44 percent, this means you are constantly replacing somebody. What if you could retain those dollars and dial back those turnover numbers?

As a company, what if you could take that money and give it to your people instead of experiencing the turnover? With turnover comes retraining and the accompanying stress—along with losing customers because you do not have the same people and/or service quality your customers expect.

By saving yourself the output of this mental energy, you can better focus on other areas of your business and on recruiting and retaining the talent you need in management, sales, and other levels within the company. Everyone is important to the overall outcome for your company. You could remove turnover as a burden to yourself and the organization with a mere twenty-five cents an hour. It could change everything.

It is important to have good producers in your company, but not everybody is going to be an A-player. Not everybody wants to sit in the C-suite. Not everybody wants to be a manager. There are some people in this world who just want to go to work, work eight to five, and not take any stress home with them. We need these people who often work with their hands or do the dirty work that most of us don't want to take on.

Like Marcus Lemonis, the star of the reality series "*The Profit*," get to the front lines of your company—spend some time on the floor with your hourly workers. Find out what it truly is like. Ask them how they are feeling. Find out what is making them happy. Find out what is important to them. Where do they shop? Do they have a family? There will always be hourly workers, so make sure you know what is important for your people and give it to them. The happy employees will be easier to retain, and you will, in turn, more easily retain the customers they serve.

Hold On to Tenured Employees

Bersin, the research division of Deloitte and Touche, addresses the importance of having tenured people in your company who are more highly skilled. They retain the institutional knowledge of the company. They build on internal and external relationships to get things done over time. Tenured employees have the confidence and rapport to improve and suggest change that new people or short-term people are unable to do for a company. These are all important points for retaining your employees that all impact the bottom line of your company.

The high cost of turnover includes a steep learning curve for new employees, along with the cost of searching and hiring, plus the loss of productivity. The more people you can keep on board beyond a year, the more they can produce for the company by way of client relations, great ideas, and innovations. They can be the institutional memory of the company telling you, "Hey, we tried that before, and these were the results. Maybe we should try it differently this time." They can also nurture returning customers and be an important piece of training initiatives. People who have tenure with your company understand how things work and how to get things done most efficiently and most effectively. They can naturally convey this knowledge to new employees. Indeed, there are many reasons to want to keep your people on board. Do not for a moment consider the tenured people a disposable, high-cost burden.

I am not suggesting that you keep people on board who are cancers to the organization. Those people must go. But in all good companies, there are great people who you can rely on to keep the torch burning and make sure it is passed along. Think of your company like the Olympics, a tradition dating back nearly 2,500 years. When somebody is done running with the torch, somebody else picks up the torch. That is what great employees are doing for your company overall.

Turnover is devastating to your company because you lose forward momentum. You lose tribal knowledge. It is prohibitively costly to replace somebody, in both dollar terms and in mental anguish. You want to retain customers because it is costly to lose them; the same applies to keeping your employees. Pay that extra twenty-five cents.

CHAPTER 12

Let Go to Grow

"I hire people brighter than me, and then I get out of their way."

—Lee Iacocca

"Hire people who are better than you are, then leave them to get on with it. Look for people who will aim for the remarkable, who will not settle for the routine."

—David Ogilvy

So many entrepreneurs cannot help themselves. They micromanage. Their companies are their babies, after all. However, the more you empower your people to run your company and make decisions—the more that you trust them—the more successful your company is going to be. Think of it like oxygen. Your company needs oxygen to grow. It needs creativity and room to be innovative. If you, the leader, are controlling everything, then you are going to lose out on the innovation from the very people in whom you have invested.

I know all too well that it is hard to let go. I have been leading my company since 2003, and it was just me for a while. When the company really started to take off, I hired others and started to trust them. Over time, I began to give responsibilities for certain functional pieces of the company to different members of my executive team. I have the best executive team I could ever hope for. It simply goes back to the issue of trust and allowing myself to trust my team to move the company forward.

Of course, there is the flip side of the trust. When somebody breaks the trust, you must evaluate whether that person remains a fit for your company. However, never go into things at the beginning thinking everybody is out to get you. That is no way to run a company, let alone your life.

I highly recommend that every leader, and especially entrepreneurs, read Dr. Jana Matthews's book, *Leading at the Speed of Growth*. It takes a close look at this subject of letting go, helping you understand your role as CEO and the different stages your company will go through as it grows. In the book, Matthews uses charts that let you know exactly what you should and should not be doing at certain levels within the evolution of your company.

Sweat the Small Stuff

I say sweat the small stuff—but without micromanaging! As we have all experienced, it is the small things that make a difference in our experience, as employees or customers—and it is also what creates your competitive advantage. Satisfy your customers' need for engagement and great products and/or services. It is not just business. This is personal. To win market success, you must separate yourself from the competitive herd. And you cannot do it alone.

Empower and develop employees who can lead for you. Look into your own business and your personal beliefs. Where are the inherent assumptions you should be challenging about your employees, your market, and your industry? Why do you do things the way you do? Should you focus on input or outcome? We have to make sure that we challenge those assumptions daily, or we risk tripping up the very evolution of our company—not to mention our own growth as leaders.

Do you trust your people first versus being suspicious of them? It is amazing how much better things go with both employee and client relationships when trust is assumed at the outset. (If somebody does not continue to earn your trust, then that is another conversation.) Low trust and micromanagement feed each other, and the two together create morale issues throughout a company. Begin with trust, and go from there.

As leaders, we need to make a habit of looking into ourselves deeply to make sure we are not stuck in our own filters and assumptions. It is our job to grow great leaders within our company. It is our job as business owners to make sure that we have people who are fully integrated human beings at the top. Basically, becoming a leader in a company is similar to becoming a remarkable human being. A great leader is somebody who can selflessly, perhaps through servanthood, succeed through other people with integrity, understanding, and a great appetite for giving.

I cannot talk about leadership and micromanagement without mentioning another wonderful leader I look up to in Denver— Ralph Christie, chairman of Merrick. Merrick is a large engineering firm that continues to be considered one of the best places to work in the city. Christie thinks that employee ownership made them more entrepreneurial and willing to take risks as a company. He believes, like many of us do, that there is more to life than work. Based on that philosophy, he built a great company by developing leaders who are focused not on the "me" but the "we" of creating success.

Nurture Your Company Based on Its Life Stage

Entrepreneurs do not always understand when they are micromanaging. *Not* micromanaging means that you delegate. It means trusting that people can make the right decisions, stepping in only when you need to or when they ask.

Companies begin as babies and from there grow in stages. As it grows, you must let your company out on its own. You can, of course, influence the style, but what your company grows into might be a little bit, or a lot, different from what you imagined early on.

As it grows, your company follows the evolution of a child who is initially dependent on you as a baby. Children, like companies, move to the point where they are more self-reliant—moving on their own, walking on their own, eating on their own. Then a company grows into a gangly teenager, where there are all kinds of opportunities, and you might not be quite sure where it is going. Suddenly, it is an adult, partly a result of your guidance and partly a result of outside influences.

The evolution of a person and the evolution of a company track together well. Understand that you, as the business owner, must know where you are in the stages of your company's evolution. You must respond to it and care for it, reacting to it thoughtfully. It is also important to understand that your employees will never be as motivated as you are if you are the entrepreneur and owner. They will never think the same way you do. Still, you can inspire them by embracing and unleashing their creativity and by giving them the responsibility to move the company forward, if you can get out of their way.

Not all entrepreneurs are great leaders, and definitely not all entrepreneurs are great managers. But they can still inspire the hell out of people. Whether you agree with everything certain entrepreneurs have done or left undone, you are inspired by their stamina and their energy and their resilience to overcome the multitude of challenges it takes to build a company.

Being a company leader or an entrepreneur is about leading into uncertainty. Isn't it remarkable that so many people run companies and jump into the fray, and they have no idea what will happen tomorrow? Anything can come their way.

September 11 changed our world, and it changed the United States of America. I, for one, will always be wondering when the next attack is going to happen. That is exactly what they wanted us to think, and it is likely to happen again at some point. I know that enough people do not like what our freedom stands for. Yet, we picked ourselves up, continued to move forward, continued to build companies and go to work, and continued to jump in. The amazing thing about American entrepreneurs is our ability to pick ourselves up, dust ourselves off, and start all over again. In a way, entrepreneurs are emblematic of our country, continuing to lead into uncertainty.

You should be proud of yourself and all of those whom you lead.

CHAPTER 13

Find Your Perfect Match

J ane was jazzed by chaos. Some said she was a thrill seeker. She was
especially so at work and in a good way. She was a thrill-seeking,
engaged job seeker looking for the dynamism of a high-growth company,
where she could wear many hats and grow her own skills as the company
expanded. Each new day's challenge was something she relished.

Companies today are in a state of constant change. Every quarter,
they are changing something within their organization to appeal to
current or new customers. The people who work in these entrepreneurial environments must be exceedingly comfortable with rapid
change. The irony, of course, is that as humans, whether a millennial,
Gen Xer, or baby boomer, are not wired for constant change. This
is a continuous source of turmoil and tension within any company.

With talent acquisition, candidates want to have a perception of security. When an environment is constantly changing, that sense of security is elusive at best. The question for a company becomes, how do you screen for the right people to work within that environment? The people you need love change and thrive in an environment of chaos. Are you interviewing people who have that DNA—people who are comfortable in the morning focusing on marketing and in the afternoon focusing on sales? If the person you are employing does not thrive on change and innovation and you are a high-innovation, rapidly changing, high-growth company, then that person will never work out for you.

Seek People Who Are "Jazzed by Chaos"

At TalenTrust we use this term: "Jazzed by Chaos." It refers to someone who is fully engaged because he or she is doing something different, new, and exciting. It is valuable for a company to have employees with a kinetic nature because they innovate and participate eagerly in the new ideas of the company. This is, however, a particular kind of person. It is not somebody who wants to punch a time clock and work from eight to five. As a company, you must screen for people who are jazzed by chaos and unpredictable environments. No day in and day out for them. These are the people who do not want to go out and be the entrepreneur themselves—perhaps not yet, anyway.

Now, let us be clear here. Successful companies need diversity in their employee populations. Everyone is important: the assembly workers; the analysts; the accountants; the people who function best by doing the same kinds of things every day, providing an underlying stability that supports the constant change. It is a matter of finding the right balance.

High-growth companies are necessarily entrepreneurial and innovative, but they do not always have processes and procedures in place. When evolving a company on the fly, it is indeed a difficult process to create and maintain a system where none existed before. You must think through each protocol before it is established and make certain you have the right people on staff to support them.

I have the distinct pleasure of serving on the board of directors for Colorado Companies to Watch. In June every year, we honor fifty high-growth companies. They represent exceptional job and revenue creation, and it is really quite amazing to be in the company of all these folks. The companies considered "Colorado Companies to Watch" are innovators. They are the companies that ask "why not?" instead of "why?" They are the people who believe in the idea of a sunrise—that there is always something new around the corner. In Mahatmas Gandhi's words, "First they'll ignore you, then they laugh at you, then they fight you, and then you win." These are the kinds of companies that we honor each year. They never give up in the face of adversity.

As an entrepreneur or expanding business leader, I am sure you recognize these words and the feelings they represent. You risk everything. Why are you doing it? You and the hundreds of Colorado Companies to Watch are brave. You and they try so many different things, so many different strategies to succeed. You are our future.

I have found through my work with Colorado Companies to Watch and TalenTrust that the people who care the most really are the crazy ones. I agree with Penny Lewandowski, who leads entrepreneurship programs for the Edward Lowe Foundation: that entrepreneurs are crazy in a good way. There is a passion to win in the DNA of an entrepreneur, which makes you a little bit crazy.

To fulfill your dream though, you need employees who are just as passionate—people who are jazzed by chaos. You both win together.

Conclusion

"People are my most important asset. 'Human Resources' isn't a thing we do. It's the thing that runs our business."

—Steve Wynn

I f your people are really your most important asset, then start acting like it. This is my number-one piece of advice to companies.

Employees hear this all the time from upper management, "People are our most important asset." Often, it is said simply because it is the right thing to say. The question is, what actions are these employers putting behind that statement to make sure their employees are engaged? What are they doing daily to make sure that people understand and are attached to their purpose?

Imagine that your company manufactures a widget for Black Hawk helicopters that are flown by our military. Can your employees draw a line from their role in making a precision widget to the helicopter where the widget must fit perfectly? Are you making sure that line is drawn in such a way that people understand that lives are at stake based on the quality of work they are performing?

I had the honor of hearing Bud Ahearn, the retired vice-chairman of CH2M HILL and former Air Force major general, speak on leadership. I love everything he represents. As an industry leader and as a military leader, he has given great advice and, in concluding this book, I would like to share a bit of his wisdom with you:

- People will break stuff, and you, as a leader, must learn to forgive them. Let people make mistakes in your company.

Find out what people stand for as well as what you stand for. Ahearn challenged us to think about how to build a company that would last for a hundred years. He argued, in his lovely way, that those are important principles of building a great company.

- He also shared that you, as a business owner, are the hero of heroes. Quite simply, the world needs more heroes like all of us, who courageously go out and try to create and expand businesses.

- As entrepreneurs and employers, we are responsible for people and their livelihoods. It is paramount that we do not lose sight of that. These are important responsibilities we have for our people. They and their children and their children's children are counting on us to do a good job for them.

When TalenTrust marked our ten-year anniversary, I reflected on my key learnings, which are still relevant today as we approach the fifteen-year mark:

- Treat everyone, not just your customers, with respect and dignity.

- Be transparent and honest in everything you do and say.

- Invest in exceptional people, and do not be cheap with anyone or anything.

- Values matter, and living them shows you are authentic. As my brother Kevin says, always do the right thing. It is not always easy, but if you do try to do the right thing, it will be good for you.

- Be humble; it is never all about you. Surround yourself with amazing people who can give you advice and help you. Get mentors, and make friends. Be a mentor.

- Grow carefully, too. Do not grow for growth's sake. Be purposeful.

- Take care of yourself. As my Daddy says, if you do not have your health, you do not have your wealth.

- Spend time with people you love. Most importantly, when you pass on, you will not be remembered for your business achievements. I know my family will remember me for being a good person, for loving them, for going to my boy's baseball games, and for going scuba diving with my husband. That is what matters most at the end of the day.

"Our deepest fear is not that we are inadequate. Our deepest fear is that we are powerful beyond measure. It is our light, not our darkness that most frightens us. We ask ourselves, Who am I to be brilliant, gorgeous, talented, and fabulous? Actually, who are you not to be? You are a child of God. Your playing small does not serve the world. There is nothing enlightened about shrinking so that other people will not feel insecure around you. We are all meant to shine, as children do. We were born to make manifest the glory of God that is within us. It is not just in some of us; it is in everyone, and as we let our own light shine, we unconsciously give others permission to do the same. As we are liberated from our own fear, our presence automatically liberates others."[30]

—Marianne Williamson

---

30 Wikiquote, "Marianne Williamson," August 19, 2015, https://en.wikiquote.org/wiki/Marianne_Williamson.

People Puzzle™ Diagnostic
Critical Talent Imperative

Based on extensive research across industries, Deloitte has identified nine fundamental talent imperatives that must be addressed in today's business environment. The goal is not to find innovative new solutions for each imperative, but to prioritize them according to your organization's needs and then develop holistic, targeted solutions that drive desired outcomes.

How well do you provide the following?

	not well		moderately well		very well	indicate priority:
	1	2	3	4	5	1= highest
Improving Speed & Quality of Hire						
Assessing & Improving Corporate Culture						
Delivering & Managing Employment Brand						
Accelerating Time to Competency						
Driving Engagement & Retention						
Planning & Analyzing Talent						
Driving Performance & Development						
Improving Management & Leadership						
Improving Career & Talent Mobility						

Simply Irresistible

Meaningful Work	Great Management	Fantastic Environment	Growth Opportunity	Trust in Leadership
• Autonomy • Selection to Fit • Small Teams • Time for Slack	• Agile Goal Setting • Coaching & Feedback • Leadership Development • Modernized Performance Mgt.	• Flexible, humane work environment • Recognition rich culture • Open flexible work spaces • Inclusive, diverse culture	• Facilitated talent mobility • Career growth in many paths • Self & formal development • High impact learning culture	• Mission and purpose • Investment in people, trust • Transparency & communication • Inspiration

New Deloitte Global Human Capital Research shows that organizations today must work hard to create a meaningful, humane work environment to drive candidate attraction and employee engagement.

How well do you provide the following?

	not well 1	2	moderately well 3	4	very well 5	indicate priority: 1= highest
Meaningful Work						
Great Management						
Fantastic Environment						
Growth Opportunity						
Trust in Leadership						

Additional Questions

Beyond your immediate recruiting needs, what people- or talent-related issues are most critical at your organization?

The economy is shifting; candidates are now in the driver's seat. How is your organization reacting to this change?

What's your overall hiring philosophy? Do you only hire on-demand for specific open roles or do you seek people with talent and fit, and then create roles for them?

What process do you have in place to treat talent acquisition like client acquisition? How do you ensure it's consistent throughout your organization?

What other concerns or issues do you have, which haven't yet been discussed?

Details
Talent Imperatives

- **Improving Speed & Quality of Hire:** Reducing the time to fill open positions helps your organization maintain optimum productivity levels. However, high quality hires are also critical to success. Research shows that the costs of hiring and onboarding can amount to ½-2/3 of the salary of a senior employee.

- **Assessing & Improving Corporate Culture:** Create a culture of choice at your organization through communication, appreciation, feedback, and balance. Once you have a clearly defined culture, you can hire people who align with your organization and drive performance.

- **Delivering & Managing Employment Brand:** Employees are your brand advocates. They will communicate this brand, so ensure the effect is positive by building a brand that people want to be a part of and share with others.

- **Accelerating Time to Competency:** Loss of productivity and a diminished learning curve of the new employees are two of the highest ranked challenges organizations face when hiring a new employee. Not only does the new employee experience low productivity, but they also decrease the productivity of those training them.

- **Driving Engagement and Retention:** As predicted in the 2014 Global Human Capital Trends report, retention and engagement remain the number two issues around the world, creating a whole new focus on employee wellness and happiness as an HR strategy.

- **Planning & Analyzing Talent:** Organizations that have a complete understanding and representation of their workforce's skills and efforts can use this information to plan for the future.

- **Driving Performance & Development:** The annual performance appraisal is becoming obsolete. Many organizations are struggling to restructure their performance management process.

- **Improving Management & Leadership:** Soon, millennials will lead a majority of the world's organizations, but few current leaders feel that they are ready for the challenge. Leadership development must be integrated with other talent initiatives to ensure success in your organizations future.

- **Improving Career & Talent Mobility:** Talent is highly mobile in today's workforce and people desire career mobility. Talent acquisition can also be greatly affected by talent mobility.

Simply Irresistible

- **Meaningful Work:** Jobs must give people enough autonomy to be creative and enough time to perform well. In todays' economy nearly every business drives value through service, intellectual property, or creativity. This means people are the product, so businesses should try to design jobs which give people what author Daniel Pink calls "autonomy, mastery, and purpose."

- **Great Management:** Management is one of the most important parts of any organization, and companies have to develop and support great leadership. Deloitte research shows that people thrive through coaching, feedback, and opportunities to develop.

- **Growth Opportunity:** Among the many reasons people leave companies, one of the biggest is for lack of opportunity. Deloitte research clearly shows that organizations that invest more heavily in training, career development, and mobility outperform their peers in almost every industry.

- **Fantastic Environment:** Companies that have ping pong tables, free food, and flexible vacation time show that they care.

- **Trust in Leadership:** CEOs now realize that it's the soul of the business that inspires people to contribute. Does your company have a mission you can relate to? Do your leaders trust employees to make the right decisions?